Henry V by William Shakespeare

The life of William Shakespeare, arguably the most significant figure in the Western literary canon, is relatively unknown.

Shakespeare was born in Stratford-upon-Avon in 1565, possibly on the 23rd April, St. George's Day, and baptised there on 26th April.

Little is known of his education and the first firm facts to his life relate to his marriage, aged 18, to Anne Hathaway, who was 26 and from the nearby village of Shottery. Anne gave birth to their first son six months later.

Shakespeare's first play, The Comedy of Errors began a procession of real heavyweights that were to emanate from his pen in a career of just over twenty years in which 37 plays were written and his reputation forever established.

This early skill was recognised by many and by 1594 the Lord Chamberlain's Men were performing his works. With the advantage of Shakespeare's progressive writing they rapidly became London's leading company of players, affording him more exposure and, following the death of Queen Elizabeth in 1603, a royal patent by the new king, James I, at which point they changed their name to the King's Men.

By 1598, and despite efforts to pirate his work, Shakespeare's name was well known and had become a selling point in its own right on title pages.

No plays are attributed to Shakespeare after 1613, and the last few plays he wrote before this time were in collaboration with other writers, one of whom is likely to be John Fletcher who succeeded him as the house playwright for the King's Men.

William Shakespeare died two months later on April 23rd, 1616, survived by his wife, two daughters and a legacy of writing that none have since yet eclipsed.

Index of Contents
DRAMATIS PERSONAE
ACT I
Prologue
Scene I - London. An Ante-Chamber in the King's Palace.
Scene II - The Came. The Presence Chamber.
ACT II
Prologue
Scene I - London. A street.
Scene II - Southampton. A Council Chamber.
Scene III - London. Before a Tavern.
Scene IV - France. The King's Palace.
ACT III
Prologue
Scene I: France. Before Harfleur.
Scene II: The Same.
Scene III: The Same. Before the Gates.

Scene IV: The French King's Palace.
Scene V: The Same.
Scene VI: The English camp in Picardy.
Scene VII: The French camp, near Agincourt:
ACT IV
Prologue
Scene I - The English Camp at Agincourt.
Scene II - The French Camp.
Scene III - The English Camp.
Scene IV - The Field of battle.
Scene V - Another Part of the Field.
Scene VI - Another Part of the Field.
Scene VII - Another Part of the Field.
Scene VIII - Before King Henry's Pavilion.
ACT V
Prologue
Scene I - France. The English Camp.
Scene II - France. A Royal Palace.
EPILOGUE
William Shakespeare – A Short Biography
William Shakespeare – A Concise Bibliography
Shakespeare; or, the Poet by Ralph Waldo Emerson
William Shakespeare – A Tribute in Verse

DRAMATIS PERSONAE
KING HENRY THE FIFTH.
DUKE OF GLOUCESTER, & DUKE OF BEDFORD: Brothers to the King.
DUKE OF EXETER, Uncle to the King.
DUKE OF YORK, Cousin to the King.
EARLS OF SALISBURY, WESTMORELAND, and WARWICK.
ARCHBISHOP OF CANTERBURY.
BISHOP OF ELY.
EARL OF CAMBRIDGE.
LORD SCROOP.
SIR THOMAS GREY.
SIR THOMAS ERPINGHAM, GOWER, FLUELLEN, MACMORRIS, & JAMY: Officers in King Henry's Army.
BATES, COURT, & WILLIAMS: Soldiers in the Same.
PISTOL, NYM, BARDOLPH.
Boy.
A Herald.
CHARLES THE SIXTH, King of France.
LEWIS, the Dauphin.
DUKES OF BURGUNDY, ORLEANS, and BOURBON.
The CONSTABLE OF FRANCE.
RAMBURES and GRANDPRÉ, French Lords.
MONTJOY, a French Herald.
Governor of Harfleur.
Ambassadors to the King of England.

ISABEL, Queen of France.
KATHARINE, Daughter to Charles and Isabel.
ALICE, a Lady attending on the Princess Katharine.
Hostess of the Boar's Head Tavern, formerly Mistress Quickly, and now married to Pistol.
Lords, Ladies, Officers, French and English Soldiers, Citizens, Messengers, and Attendants.

Chorus.

SCENE.—England; afterwards France.

ACT I

PROLOGUE

Enter CHORUS

CHORUS
O for a Muse of fire, that would ascend
The brightest heaven of invention,
A kingdom for a stage, princes to act
And monarchs to behold the swelling scene!
Then should the warlike Harry, like himself,
Assume the port of Mars; and at his heels,
Leash'd in like hounds, should famine, sword and fire
Crouch for employment. But pardon, and gentles all,
The flat unraised spirits that have dared
On this unworthy scaffold to bring forth
So great an object: can this cockpit hold
The vasty fields of France? or may we cram
Within this wooden O the very casques
That did affright the air at Agincourt?
O, pardon! since a crooked figure may
Attest in little place a million;
And let us, ciphers to this great accompt,
On your imaginary forces work.
Suppose within the girdle of these walls
Are now confined two mighty monarchies,
Whose high upreared and abutting fronts
The perilous narrow ocean parts asunder:
Piece out our imperfections with your thoughts;
Into a thousand parts divide on man,
And make imaginary puissance;
Think when we talk of horses, that you see them
Printing their proud hoofs i' the receiving earth;
For 'tis your thoughts that now must deck our kings,
Carry them here and there; jumping o'er times,
Turning the accomplishment of many years

Into an hour-glass: for the which supply,
Admit me Chorus to this history;
Who prologue-like your humble patience pray,
Gently to hear, kindly to judge, our play.

Exit

SCENE I. London. An Ante-Chamber in the King's Palace

Enter the ARCHBISHOP OF CANTERBURY, and the BISHOP OF ELY

CANTERBURY
My lord, I'll tell you; that self bill is urged,
Which in the eleventh year of the last king's reign
Was like, and had indeed against us pass'd,
But that the scambling and unquiet time
Did push it out of farther question.

ELY
But how, my lord, shall we resist it now?

CANTERBURY
It must be thought on. If it pass against us,
We lose the better half of our possession:
For all the temporal lands which men devout
By testament have given to the church
Would they strip from us; being valued thus:
As much as would maintain, to the king's honour,
Full fifteen earls and fifteen hundred knights,
Six thousand and two hundred good esquires;
And, to relief of lazars and weak age,
Of indigent faint souls past corporal toil.
A hundred almshouses right well supplied;
And to the coffers of the king beside,
A thousand pounds by the year: thus runs the bill.

ELY
This would drink deep.

CANTERBURY
'Twould drink the cup and all.

ELY
But what prevention?

CANTERBURY
The king is full of grace and fair regard.

ELY

And a true lover of the holy church.

CANTERBURY
The courses of his youth promised it not.
The breath no sooner left his father's body,
But that his wildness, mortified in him,
Seem'd to die too; yea, at that very moment
Consideration, like an angel, came
And whipp'd the offending Adam out of him,
Leaving his body as a paradise,
To envelop and contain celestial spirits.
Never was such a sudden scholar made;
Never came reformation in a flood,
With such a heady currance, scouring faults
Nor never Hydra-headed wilfulness
So soon did lose his seat and all at once
As in this king.

ELY
We are blessed in the change.

CANTERBURY
Hear him but reason in divinity,
And all-admiring with an inward wish
You would desire the king were made a prelate:
Hear him debate of commonwealth affairs,
You would say it hath been all in all his study:
List his discourse of war, and you shall hear
A fearful battle render'd you in music:
Turn him to any cause of policy,
The Gordian knot of it he will unloose,
Familiar as his garter: that, when he speaks,
The air, a charter'd libertine, is still,
And the mute wonder lurketh in men's ears,
To steal his sweet and honey'd sentences;
So that the art and practic part of life
Must be the mistress to this theoric:
Which is a wonder how his grace should glean it,
Since his addiction was to courses vain,
His companies unletter'd, rude and shallow,
His hours fill'd up with riots, banquets, sports,
And never noted in him any study,
Any retirement, any sequestration
From open haunts and popularity.

ELY
The strawberry grows underneath the nettle
And wholesome berries thrive and ripen best
Neighbour'd by fruit of baser quality:
And so the prince obscured his contemplation
Under the veil of wildness; which, no doubt,

Grew like the summer grass, fastest by night,
Unseen, yet crescive in his faculty.

CANTERBURY
It must be so; for miracles are ceased;
And therefore we must needs admit the means
How things are perfected.

ELY
But, my good lord,
How now for mitigation of this bill
Urged by the commons? Doth his majesty
Incline to it, or no?

CANTERBURY
He seems indifferent,
Or rather swaying more upon our part
Than cherishing the exhibiters against us;
For I have made an offer to his majesty,
Upon our spiritual convocation
And in regard of causes now in hand,
Which I have open'd to his grace at large,
As touching France, to give a greater sum
Than ever at one time the clergy yet
Did to his predecessors part withal.

ELY
How did this offer seem received, my lord?

CANTERBURY
With good acceptance of his majesty;
Save that there was not time enough to hear,
As I perceived his grace would fain have done,
The severals and unhidden passages
Of his true titles to some certain dukedoms
And generally to the crown and seat of France
Derived from Edward, his great-grandfather.

ELY
What was the impediment that broke this off?

CANTERBURY
The French ambassador upon that instant
Craved audience; and the hour, I think, is come
To give him hearing: is it four o'clock?

ELY
It is.

CANTERBURY

Then go we in, to know his embassy;
Which I could with a ready guess declare,
Before the Frenchman speak a word of it.

ELY
I'll wait upon you, and I long to hear it.

Exeunt

SCENE II. The Same. The Presence Chamber

Enter KING HENRY V, GLOUCESTER, BEDFORD, EXETER, WARWICK, WESTMORELAND, and Attendants

KING HENRY V
Where is my gracious Lord of Canterbury?

EXETER
Not here in presence.

KING HENRY V
Send for him, good uncle.

WESTMORELAND
Shall we call in the ambassador, my liege?

KING HENRY V
Not yet, my cousin: we would be resolved,
Before we hear him, of some things of weight
That task our thoughts, concerning us and France.

Enter the ARCHBISHOP OF CANTERBURY, and the BISHOP of ELY

CANTERBURY
God and his angels guard your sacred throne
And make you long become it!

KING HENRY V
Sure, we thank you.
My learned lord, we pray you to proceed
And justly and religiously unfold
Why the law Salique that they have in France
Or should, or should not, bar us in our claim:
And God forbid, my dear and faithful lord,
That you should fashion, wrest, or bow your reading,
Or nicely charge your understanding soul
With opening titles miscreate, whose right
Suits not in native colours with the truth;
For God doth know how many now in health
Shall drop their blood in approbation

Of what your reverence shall incite us to.
Therefore take heed how you impawn our person,
How you awake our sleeping sword of war:
We charge you, in the name of God, take heed;
For never two such kingdoms did contend
Without much fall of blood; whose guiltless drops
Are every one a woe, a sore complaint
'Gainst him whose wrong gives edge unto the swords
That make such waste in brief mortality.
Under this conjuration, speak, my lord;
For we will hear, note and believe in heart
That what you speak is in your conscience wash'd
As pure as sin with baptism.

CANTERBURY
Then hear me, gracious sovereign, and you peers,
That owe yourselves, your lives and services
To this imperial throne. There is no bar
To make against your highness' claim to France
But this, which they produce from Pharamond,
'In terram Salicam mulieres ne succedant:'
'No woman shall succeed in Salique land:'
Which Salique land the French unjustly gloze
To be the realm of France, and Pharamond
The founder of this law and female bar.
Yet their own authors faithfully affirm
That the land Salique is in Germany,
Between the floods of Sala and of Elbe;
Where Charles the Great, having subdued the Saxons,
There left behind and settled certain French;
Who, holding in disdain the German women
For some dishonest manners of their life,
Establish'd then this law; to wit, no female
Should be inheritrix in Salique land:
Which Salique, as I said, 'twixt Elbe and Sala,
Is at this day in Germany call'd Meisen.
Then doth it well appear that Salique law
Was not devised for the realm of France:
Nor did the French possess the Salique land
Until four hundred one and twenty years
After defunction of King Pharamond,
Idly supposed the founder of this law;
Who died within the year of our redemption
Four hundred twenty-six; and Charles the Great
Subdued the Saxons, and did seat the French
Beyond the river Sala, in the year
Eight hundred five. Besides, their writers say,
King Pepin, which deposed Childeric,
Did, as heir general, being descended
Of Blithild, which was daughter to King Clothair,
Make claim and title to the crown of France.

Hugh Capet also, who usurped the crown
Of Charles the duke of Lorraine, sole heir male
Of the true line and stock of Charles the Great,
To find his title with some shows of truth,
'Through, in pure truth, it was corrupt and naught,
Convey'd himself as heir to the Lady Lingare,
Daughter to Charlemain, who was the son
To Lewis the emperor, and Lewis the son
Of Charles the Great. Also King Lewis the Tenth,
Who was sole heir to the usurper Capet,
Could not keep quiet in his conscience,
Wearing the crown of France, till satisfied
That fair Queen Isabel, his grandmother,
Was lineal of the Lady Ermengare,
Daughter to Charles the foresaid duke of Lorraine:
By the which marriage the line of Charles the Great
Was re-united to the crown of France.
So that, as clear as is the summer's sun.
King Pepin's title and Hugh Capet's claim,
King Lewis his satisfaction, all appear
To hold in right and title of the female:
So do the kings of France unto this day;
Howbeit they would hold up this Salique law
To bar your highness claiming from the female,
And rather choose to hide them in a net
Than amply to imbar their crooked titles
Usurp'd from you and your progenitors.

KING HENRY V
May I with right and conscience make this claim?

CANTERBURY
The sin upon my head, dread sovereign!
For in the book of Numbers is it writ,
When the man dies, let the inheritance
Descend unto the daughter. Gracious lord,
Stand for your own; unwind your bloody flag;
Look back into your mighty ancestors:
Go, my dread lord, to your great-grandsire's tomb,
From whom you claim; invoke his warlike spirit,
And your great-uncle's, Edward the Black Prince,
Who on the French ground play'd a tragedy,
Making defeat on the full power of France,
Whiles his most mighty father on a hill
Stood smiling to behold his lion's whelp
Forage in blood of French nobility.
O noble English. that could entertain
With half their forces the full Pride of France
And let another half stand laughing by,
All out of work and cold for action!

ELY
Awake remembrance of these valiant dead
And with your puissant arm renew their feats:
You are their heir; you sit upon their throne;
The blood and courage that renowned them
Runs in your veins; and my thrice-puissant liege
Is in the very May-morn of his youth,
Ripe for exploits and mighty enterprises.

EXETER
Your brother kings and monarchs of the earth
Do all expect that you should rouse yourself,
As did the former lions of your blood.

WESTMORELAND
They know your grace hath cause and means and might;
So hath your highness; never king of England
Had nobles richer and more loyal subjects,
Whose hearts have left their bodies here in England
And lie pavilion'd in the fields of France.

CANTERBURY
O, let their bodies follow, my dear liege,
With blood and sword and fire to win your right;
In aid whereof we of the spiritualty
Will raise your highness such a mighty sum
As never did the clergy at one time
Bring in to any of your ancestors.

KING HENRY V
We must not only arm to invade the French,
But lay down our proportions to defend
Against the Scot, who will make road upon us
With all advantages.

CANTERBURY
They of those marches, gracious sovereign,
Shall be a wall sufficient to defend
Our inland from the pilfering borderers.

KING HENRY V
We do not mean the coursing snatchers only,
But fear the main intendment of the Scot,
Who hath been still a giddy neighbour to us;
For you shall read that my great-grandfather
Never went with his forces into France
But that the Scot on his unfurnish'd kingdom
Came pouring, like the tide into a breach,
With ample and brim fulness of his force,
Galling the gleaned land with hot assays,
Girding with grievous siege castles and towns;

That England, being empty of defence,
Hath shook and trembled at the ill neighbourhood.

CANTERBURY
She hath been then more fear'd than harm'd, my liege;
For hear her but exampled by herself:
When all her chivalry hath been in France
And she a mourning widow of her nobles,
She hath herself not only well defended
But taken and impounded as a stray
The King of Scots; whom she did send to France,
To fill King Edward's fame with prisoner kings
And make her chronicle as rich with praise
As is the ooze and bottom of the sea
With sunken wreck and sunless treasuries.

WESTMORELAND
But there's a saying very old and true,
'If that you will France win,
Then with Scotland first begin:'
For once the eagle England being in prey,
To her unguarded nest the weasel Scot
Comes sneaking and so sucks her princely eggs,
Playing the mouse in absence of the cat,
To tear and havoc more than she can eat.

EXETER
It follows then the cat must stay at home:
Yet that is but a crush'd necessity,
Since we have locks to safeguard necessaries,
And pretty traps to catch the petty thieves.
While that the armed hand doth fight abroad,
The advised head defends itself at home;
For government, though high and low and lower,
Put into parts, doth keep in one consent,
Congreeing in a full and natural close,
Like music.

CANTERBURY
Therefore doth heaven divide
The state of man in divers functions,
Setting endeavour in continual motion;
To which is fixed, as an aim or butt,
Obedience: for so work the honey-bees,
Creatures that by a rule in nature teach
The act of order to a peopled kingdom.
They have a king and officers of sorts;
Where some, like magistrates, correct at home,
Others, like merchants, venture trade abroad,
Others, like soldiers, armed in their stings,
Make boot upon the summer's velvet buds,

Which pillage they with merry march bring home
To the tent-royal of their emperor;
Who, busied in his majesty, surveys
The singing masons building roofs of gold,
The civil citizens kneading up the honey,
The poor mechanic porters crowding in
Their heavy burdens at his narrow gate,
The sad-eyed justice, with his surly hum,
Delivering o'er to executors pale
The lazy yawning drone. I this infer,
That many things, having full reference
To one consent, may work contrariously:
As many arrows, loosed several ways,
Come to one mark; as many ways meet in one town;
As many fresh streams meet in one salt sea;
As many lines close in the dial's centre;
So may a thousand actions, once afoot.
End in one purpose, and be all well borne
Without defeat. Therefore to France, my liege.
Divide your happy England into four;
Whereof take you one quarter into France,
And you withal shall make all Gallia shake.
If we, with thrice such powers left at home,
Cannot defend our own doors from the dog,
Let us be worried and our nation lose
The name of hardiness and policy.

KING HENRY V
Call in the messengers sent from the Dauphin.

Exeunt some Attendants

Now are we well resolved; and, by God's help,
And yours, the noble sinews of our power,
France being ours, we'll bend it to our awe,
Or break it all to pieces: or there we'll sit,
Ruling in large and ample empery
O'er France and all her almost kingly dukedoms,
Or lay these bones in an unworthy urn,
Tombless, with no remembrance over them:
Either our history shall with full mouth
Speak freely of our acts, or else our grave,
Like Turkish mute, shall have a tongueless mouth,
Not worshipp'd with a waxen epitaph.

Enter AMBASSADORS of France

Now are we well prepared to know the pleasure
Of our fair cousin Dauphin; for we hear
Your greeting is from him, not from the king.

FIRST AMBASSADOR
May't please your majesty to give us leave
Freely to render what we have in charge;
Or shall we sparingly show you far off
The Dauphin's meaning and our embassy?

KING HENRY V
We are no tyrant, but a Christian king;
Unto whose grace our passion is as subject
As are our wretches fetter'd in our prisons:
Therefore with frank and with uncurbed plainness
Tell us the Dauphin's mind.

FIRST AMBASSADOR
Thus, then, in few.
Your highness, lately sending into France,
Did claim some certain dukedoms, in the right
Of your great predecessor, King Edward the Third.
In answer of which claim, the prince our master
Says that you savour too much of your youth,
And bids you be advised there's nought in France
That can be with a nimble galliard won;
You cannot revel into dukedoms there.
He therefore sends you, meeter for your spirit,
This tun of treasure; and, in lieu of this,
Desires you let the dukedoms that you claim
Hear no more of you. This the Dauphin speaks.

KING HENRY V
What treasure, uncle?

EXETER
Tennis-balls, my liege.

KING HENRY V
We are glad the Dauphin is so pleasant with us;
His present and your pains we thank you for:
When we have march'd our rackets to these balls,
We will, in France, by God's grace, play a set
Shall strike his father's crown into the hazard.
Tell him he hath made a match with such a wrangler
That all the courts of France will be disturb'd
With chaces. And we understand him well,
How he comes o'er us with our wilder days,
Not measuring what use we made of them.
We never valued this poor seat of England;
And therefore, living hence, did give ourself
To barbarous licence; as 'tis ever common
That men are merriest when they are from home.
But tell the Dauphin I will keep my state,
Be like a king and show my sail of greatness

When I do rouse me in my throne of France:
For that I have laid by my majesty
And plodded like a man for working-days,
But I will rise there with so full a glory
That I will dazzle all the eyes of France,
Yea, strike the Dauphin blind to look on us.
And tell the pleasant prince this mock of his
Hath turn'd his balls to gun-stones; and his soul
Shall stand sore charged for the wasteful vengeance
That shall fly with them: for many a thousand widows
Shall this his mock mock out of their dear husbands;
Mock mothers from their sons, mock castles down;
And some are yet ungotten and unborn
That shall have cause to curse the Dauphin's scorn.
But this lies all within the will of God,
To whom I do appeal; and in whose name
Tell you the Dauphin I am coming on,
To venge me as I may and to put forth
My rightful hand in a well-hallow'd cause.
So get you hence in peace; and tell the Dauphin
His jest will savour but of shallow wit,
When thousands weep more than did laugh at it.
Convey them with safe conduct. Fare you well.

Exeunt AMBASSADORS

EXETER
This was a merry message.

KING HENRY V
We hope to make the sender blush at it.
Therefore, my lords, omit no happy hour
That may give furtherance to our expedition;
For we have now no thought in us but France,
Save those to God, that run before our business.
Therefore let our proportions for these wars
Be soon collected and all things thought upon
That may with reasonable swiftness add
More feathers to our wings; for, God before,
We'll chide this Dauphin at his father's door.
Therefore let every man now task his thought,
That this fair action may on foot be brought.

Exeunt. Flourish

ACT II

PROLOGUE

Enter CHORUS

CHORUS
Now all the youth of England are on fire,
And silken dalliance in the wardrobe lies:
Now thrive the armourers, and honour's thought
Reigns solely in the breast of every man:
They sell the pasture now to buy the horse,
Following the mirror of all Christian kings,
With winged heels, as English Mercuries.
For now sits Expectation in the air,
And hides a sword from hilts unto the point
With crowns imperial, crowns and coronets,
Promised to Harry and his followers.
The French, advised by good intelligence
Of this most dreadful preparation,
Shake in their fear and with pale policy
Seek to divert the English purposes.
O England! model to thy inward greatness,
Like little body with a mighty heart,
What mightst thou do, that honour would thee do,
Were all thy children kind and natural!
But see thy fault! France hath in thee found out
A nest of hollow bosoms, which he fills
With treacherous crowns; and three corrupted men,
One, Richard Earl of Cambridge, and the second,
Henry Lord Scroop of Masham, and the third,
Sir Thomas Grey, knight, of Northumberland,
Have, for the gilt of France, O guilt indeed!
Confirm'd conspiracy with fearful France;
And by their hands this grace of kings must die,
If hell and treason hold their promises,
Ere he take ship for France, and in Southampton.
Linger your patience on; and we'll digest
The abuse of distance; force a play:
The sum is paid; the traitors are agreed;
The king is set from London; and the scene
Is now transported, gentles, to Southampton;
There is the playhouse now, there must you sit:
And thence to France shall we convey you safe,
And bring you back, charming the narrow seas
To give you gentle pass; for, if we may,
We'll not offend one stomach with our play.
But, till the king come forth, and not till then,
Unto Southampton do we shift our scene.

Exit

SCENE I. London. A Street

Enter Corporal NYM and Lieutenant BARDOLPH

BARDOLPH
Well met, Corporal Nym.

NYM
Good morrow, Lieutenant Bardolph.

BARDOLPH
What, are Ancient Pistol and you friends yet?

NYM
For my part, I care not: I say little; but when time shall serve, there shall be smiles; but that shall be as it may. I dare not fight; but I will wink and hold out mine iron: it is a simple one; but what though? it will toast cheese, and it will endure cold as another man's sword will: and there's an end.

BARDOLPH
I will bestow a breakfast to make you friends; and we'll be all three sworn brothers to France: let it be so, good Corporal Nym.

NYM
Faith, I will live so long as I may, that's the certain of it; and when I cannot live any longer, I will do as I may: that is my rest, that is the rendezvous of it.

BARDOLPH
It is certain, corporal, that he is married to Nell Quickly: and certainly she did you wrong; for you were troth-plight to her.

NYM
I cannot tell: things must be as they may: men may sleep, and they may have their throats about them at that time; and some say knives have edges. It must be as it may: though patience be a tired mare, yet she will plod. There must be conclusions. Well, I cannot tell.

Enter PISTOL and HOSTESS

BARDOLPH
Here comes Ancient Pistol and his wife: good corporal, be patient here. How now, mine host Pistol!

PISTOL
Base tike, call'st thou me host? Now, by this hand, I swear, I scorn the term; Nor shall my Nell keep lodgers.

HOSTESS
No, by my troth, not long; for we cannot lodge and board a dozen or fourteen gentlewomen that live honestly by the prick of their needles, but it will be thought we keep a bawdy house straight.

NYM and PISTOL draw

O well a day, Lady, if he be not drawn now! We shall see wilful adultery and murder committed.

BARDOLPH
Good lieutenant! good corporal! offer nothing here.

NYM
Pish!

PISTOL
Pish for thee, Iceland dog! thou prick-ear'd cur of Iceland!

HOSTESS
Good Corporal Nym, show thy valour, and put up your sword.

NYM
Will you shog off? I would have you solus.

PISTOL
'Solus,' egregious dog? O viper vile!
The 'solus' in thy most mervailous face;
The 'solus' in thy teeth, and in thy throat,
And in thy hateful lungs, yea, in thy maw, perdy,
And, which is worse, within thy nasty mouth!
I do retort the 'solus' in thy bowels;
For I can take, and Pistol's cock is up,
And flashing fire will follow.

NYM
I am not Barbason; you cannot conjure me. I have an humour to knock you indifferently well. If you grow foul with me, Pistol, I will scour you with my rapier, as I may, in fair terms: if you would walk off, I would prick your guts a little, in good terms, as I may: and that's the humour of it.

PISTOL
O braggart vile and damned furious wight!
The grave doth gape, and doting death is near;
Therefore exhale.

BARDOLPH
Hear me, hear me what I say: he that strikes the first stroke, I'll run him up to the hilts, as I am a soldier.

Draws

PISTOL
An oath of mickle might; and fury shall abate.
Give me thy fist, thy fore-foot to me give:
Thy spirits are most tall.

NYM
I will cut thy throat, one time or other, in fair terms: that is the humour of it.

PISTOL

'Couple a gorge!'
That is the word. I thee defy again.
O hound of Crete, think'st thou my spouse to get?
No; to the spital go,
And from the powdering tub of infamy
Fetch forth the lazar kite of Cressid's kind,
Doll Tearsheet she by name, and her espouse:
I have, and I will hold, the quondam Quickly
For the only she; and—pauca, there's enough. Go to.

Enter the BOY

BOY
Mine host Pistol, you must come to my master, and you, hostess: he is very sick, and would to bed. Good Bardolph, put thy face between his sheets, and do the office of a warming-pan. Faith, he's very ill.

BARDOLPH
Away, you rogue!

HOSTESS
By my troth, he'll yield the crow a pudding one of these days. The king has killed his heart. Good husband, come home presently.

Exeunt HOSTESS and BOY

BARDOLPH
Come, shall I make you two friends? We must to France together: why the devil should we keep knives to cut one another's throats?

PISTOL
Let floods o'erswell, and fiends for food howl on!

NYM
You'll pay me the eight shillings I won of you at betting?

PISTOL
Base is the slave that pays.

NYM
That now I will have: that's the humour of it.

PISTOL
As manhood shall compound: push home.

They draw

BARDOLPH
By this sword, he that makes the first thrust, I'll kill him; by this sword, I will.

PISTOL

Sword is an oath, and oaths must have their course.

BARDOLPH
Corporal Nym, an thou wilt be friends, be friends: an thou wilt not, why, then, be enemies with me too. Prithee, put up.

NYM
I shall have my eight shillings I won of you at betting?

PISTOL
A noble shalt thou have, and present pay;
And liquor likewise will I give to thee,
And friendship shall combine, and brotherhood:
I'll live by Nym, and Nym shall live by me;
Is not this just? for I shall sutler be
Unto the camp, and profits will accrue.
Give me thy hand.

NYM
I shall have my noble?

PISTOL
In cash most justly paid.

NYM
Well, then, that's the humour of't.

Re-enter HOSTESS

HOSTESS
As ever you came of women, come in quickly to Sir John. Ah, poor heart! he is so shaked of a burning quotidian tertian, that it is most lamentable to behold. Sweet men, come to him.

NYM
The king hath run bad humours on the knight; that's the even of it.

PISTOL
Nym, thou hast spoke the right;
His heart is fracted and corroborate.

NYM
The king is a good king: but it must be as it may; he passes some humours and careers.

PISTOL
Let us condole the knight; for, lambkins we will live.

SCENE II. Southampton. A Council Chamber

Enter EXETER, BEDFORD, and WESTMORELAND

BEDFORD
'Fore God, his grace is bold, to trust these traitors.

EXETER
They shall be apprehended by and by.

WESTMORELAND
How smooth and even they do bear themselves!
As if allegiance in their bosoms sat,
Crowned with faith and constant loyalty.

BEDFORD
The king hath note of all that they intend,
By interception which they dream not of.

EXETER
Nay, but the man that was his bedfellow,
Whom he hath dull'd and cloy'd with gracious favours,
That he should, for a foreign purse, so sell
His sovereign's life to death and treachery.

Trumpets sound.

Enter KING HENRY V, SCROOP, CAMBRIDGE, GREY, and Attendants

KING HENRY V
Now sits the wind fair, and we will aboard.
My Lord of Cambridge, and my kind Lord of Masham,
And you, my gentle knight, give me your thoughts:
Think you not that the powers we bear with us
Will cut their passage through the force of France,
Doing the execution and the act
For which we have in head assembled them?

SCROOP
No doubt, my liege, if each man do his best.

KING HENRY V
I doubt not that; since we are well persuaded
We carry not a heart with us from hence
That grows not in a fair consent with ours,
Nor leave not one behind that doth not wish
Success and conquest to attend on us.

CAMBRIDGE
Never was monarch better fear'd and loved
Than is your majesty: there's not, I think, a subject
That sits in heart-grief and uneasiness
Under the sweet shade of your government.

GREY
True: those that were your father's enemies
Have steep'd their galls in honey and do serve you
With hearts create of duty and of zeal.

KING HENRY V
We therefore have great cause of thankfulness;
And shall forget the office of our hand,
Sooner than quittance of desert and merit
According to the weight and worthiness.

SCROOP
So service shall with steeled sinews toil,
And labour shall refresh itself with hope,
To do your grace incessant services.

KING HENRY V
We judge no less. Uncle of Exeter,
Enlarge the man committed yesterday,
That rail'd against our person: we consider
it was excess of wine that set him on;
And on his more advice we pardon him.

SCROOP
That's mercy, but too much security:
Let him be punish'd, sovereign, lest example
Breed, by his sufferance, more of such a kind.

KING HENRY V
O, let us yet be merciful.

CAMBRIDGE
So may your highness, and yet punish too.

GREY
Sir,
You show great mercy, if you give him life,
After the taste of much correction.

KING HENRY V
Alas, your too much love and care of me
Are heavy orisons 'gainst this poor wretch!
If little faults, proceeding on distemper,
Shall not be wink'd at, how shall we stretch our eye
When capital crimes, chew'd, swallow'd and digested,
Appear before us? We'll yet enlarge that man,
Though Cambridge, Scroop and Grey, in their dear care
And tender preservation of our person,
Would have him punished. And now to our French causes:
Who are the late commissioners?

CAMBRIDGE
I one, my lord:
Your highness bade me ask for it to-day.

SCROOP
So did you me, my liege.

GREY
And I, my royal sovereign.

KING HENRY V
Then, Richard Earl of Cambridge, there is yours;
There yours, Lord Scroop of Masham; and, sir knight,
Grey of Northumberland, this same is yours:
Read them; and know, I know your worthiness.
My Lord of Westmoreland, and uncle Exeter,
We will aboard to night. Why, how now, gentlemen!
What see you in those papers that you lose
So much complexion? Look ye, how they change!
Their cheeks are paper. Why, what read you there
That hath so cowarded and chased your blood
Out of appearance?

CAMBRIDGE
I do confess my fault;
And do submit me to your highness' mercy.

GREY SCROOP
To which we all appeal.

KING HENRY V
The mercy that was quick in us but late,
By your own counsel is suppress'd and kill'd:
You must not dare, for shame, to talk of mercy;
For your own reasons turn into your bosoms,
As dogs upon their masters, worrying you.
See you, my princes, and my noble peers,
These English monsters! My Lord of Cambridge here,
You know how apt our love was to accord
To furnish him with all appertinents
Belonging to his honour; and this man
Hath, for a few light crowns, lightly conspired,
And sworn unto the practises of France,
To kill us here in Hampton: to the which
This knight, no less for bounty bound to us
Than Cambridge is, hath likewise sworn. But, O,
What shall I say to thee, Lord Scroop? thou cruel,
Ingrateful, savage and inhuman creature!
Thou that didst bear the key of all my counsels,
That knew'st the very bottom of my soul,
That almost mightst have coin'd me into gold,

Wouldst thou have practised on me for thy use,
May it be possible, that foreign hire
Could out of thee extract one spark of evil
That might annoy my finger? 'tis so strange,
That, though the truth of it stands off as gross
As black and white, my eye will scarcely see it.
Treason and murder ever kept together,
As two yoke-devils sworn to either's purpose,
Working so grossly in a natural cause,
That admiration did not whoop at them:
But thou, 'gainst all proportion, didst bring in
Wonder to wait on treason and on murder:
And whatsoever cunning fiend it was
That wrought upon thee so preposterously
Hath got the voice in hell for excellence:
All other devils that suggest by treasons
Do botch and bungle up damnation
With patches, colours, and with forms being fetch'd
From glistering semblances of piety;
But he that temper'd thee bade thee stand up,
Gave thee no instance why thou shouldst do treason,
Unless to dub thee with the name of traitor.
If that same demon that hath gull'd thee thus
Should with his lion gait walk the whole world,
He might return to vasty Tartar back,
And tell the legions 'I can never win
A soul so easy as that Englishman's.'
O, how hast thou with 'jealousy infected
The sweetness of affiance! Show men dutiful?
Why, so didst thou: seem they grave and learned?
Why, so didst thou: come they of noble family?
Why, so didst thou: seem they religious?
Why, so didst thou: or are they spare in diet,
Free from gross passion or of mirth or anger,
Constant in spirit, not swerving with the blood,
Garnish'd and deck'd in modest complement,
Not working with the eye without the ear,
And but in purged judgment trusting neither?
Such and so finely bolted didst thou seem:
And thus thy fall hath left a kind of blot,
To mark the full-fraught man and best indued
With some suspicion. I will weep for thee;
For this revolt of thine, methinks, is like
Another fall of man. Their faults are open:
Arrest them to the answer of the law;
And God acquit them of their practises!

EXETER
I arrest thee of high treason, by the name of
Richard Earl of Cambridge.
I arrest thee of high treason, by the name of

Henry Lord Scroop of Masham.
I arrest thee of high treason, by the name of
Thomas Grey, knight, of Northumberland.

SCROOP
Our purposes God justly hath discover'd;
And I repent my fault more than my death;
Which I beseech your highness to forgive,
Although my body pay the price of it.

CAMBRIDGE
For me, the gold of France did not seduce;
Although I did admit it as a motive
The sooner to effect what I intended:
But God be thanked for prevention;
Which I in sufferance heartily will rejoice,
Beseeching God and you to pardon me.

GREY
Never did faithful subject more rejoice
At the discovery of most dangerous treason
Than I do at this hour joy o'er myself.
Prevented from a damned enterprise:
My fault, but not my body, pardon, sovereign.

KING HENRY V
God quit you in his mercy! Hear your sentence.
You have conspired against our royal person,
Join'd with an enemy proclaim'd and from his coffers
Received the golden earnest of our death;
Wherein you would have sold your king to slaughter,
His princes and his peers to servitude,
His subjects to oppression and contempt
And his whole kingdom into desolation.
Touching our person seek we no revenge;
But we our kingdom's safety must so tender,
Whose ruin you have sought, that to her laws
We do deliver you. Get you therefore hence,
Poor miserable wretches, to your death:
The taste whereof, God of his mercy give
You patience to endure, and true repentance
Of all your dear offences! Bear them hence.

Exeunt CAMBRIDGE, SCROOP and GREY, guarded

Now, lords, for France; the enterprise whereof
Shall be to you, as us, like glorious.
We doubt not of a fair and lucky war,
Since God so graciously hath brought to light
This dangerous treason lurking in our way
To hinder our beginnings. We doubt not now

But every rub is smoothed on our way.
Then forth, dear countrymen: let us deliver
Our puissance into the hand of God,
Putting it straight in expedition.
Cheerly to sea; the signs of war advance:
No king of England, if not king of France.

Exeunt

SCENE III. London. Before a Tavern

Enter PISTOL, Hostess, NYM, BARDOLPH, and Boy

HOSTESS
Prithee, honey-sweet husband, let me bring thee to Staines.

PISTOL
No; for my manly heart doth yearn.
Bardolph, be blithe: Nym, rouse thy vaunting veins:
Boy, bristle thy courage up; for Falstaff he is dead,
And we must yearn therefore.

BARDOLPH
Would I were with him, wheresome'er he is, either in heaven or in hell!

HOSTESS
Nay, sure, he's not in hell: he's in Arthur's bosom, if ever man went to Arthur's bosom. A' made a finer end and went away an it had been any christom child; a' parted even just between twelve and one, even at the turning o' the tide: for after I saw him fumble with the sheets and play with flowers and smile upon his fingers' ends, I knew there was but one way; for his nose was as sharp as a pen, and a' babbled of green fields. 'How now, sir John!' quoth I 'what, man! be o' good cheer.' So a' cried out 'God, God, God!' three or four times. Now I, to comfort him, bid him a' should not think of God; I hoped there was no need to trouble himself with any such thoughts yet. So a' bade me lay more clothes on his feet: I put my hand into the bed and felt them, and they were as cold as any stone; then I felt to his knees, and they were as cold as any stone, and so upward and upward, and all was as cold as any stone.

NYM
They say he cried out of sack.

HOSTESS
Ay, that a' did.

BARDOLPH
And of women.

HOSTESS
Nay, that a' did not.

BOY
Yes, that a' did; and said they were devils incarnate.

HOSTESS
A' could never abide carnation; 'twas a colour he never liked.

BOY
A' said once, the devil would have him about women.

HOSTESS
A' did in some sort, indeed, handle women; but then he was rheumatic, and talked of the whore of Babylon.

BOY
Do you not remember, a' saw a flea stick upon Bardolph's nose, and a' said it was a black soul burning in hell-fire?

BARDOLPH
Well, the fuel is gone that maintained that fire: that's all the riches I got in his service.

NYM
Shall we shog? the king will be gone from Southampton.

PISTOL
Come, let's away. My love, give me thy lips.
Look to my chattels and my movables:
Let senses rule; the word is 'Pitch and Pay:'
Trust none;
For oaths are straws, men's faiths are wafer-cakes,
And hold-fast is the only dog, my duck:
Therefore, Caveto be thy counsellor.
Go, clear thy c rystals. Yoke-fellows in arms,
Let us to France; like horse-leeches, my boys,
To suck, to suck, the very blood to suck!

BOY
And that's but unwholesome food they say.

PISTOL
Touch her soft mouth, and march.

BARDOLPH
Farewell, hostess.

Kissing her

NYM
I cannot kiss, that is the humour of it; but, adieu.

PISTOL
Let housewifery appear: keep close, I thee command.

HOSTESS
Farewell; adieu.

Exeunt

SCENE IV. France. The King's Palace.

Flourish. Enter the FRENCH KING, the DAUPHIN, the DUKES of BERRI and BRETAGNE, the CONSTABLE, and others

KING OF FRANCE
Thus comes the English with full power upon us;
And more than carefully it us concerns
To answer royally in our defences.
Therefore the Dukes of Berri and of Bretagne,
Of Brabant and of Orleans, shall make forth,
And you, Prince Dauphin, with all swift dispatch,
To line and new repair our towns of war
With men of courage and with means defendant;
For England his approaches makes as fierce
As waters to the sucking of a gulf.
It fits us then to be as provident
As fear may teach us out of late examples
Left by the fatal and neglected English
Upon our fields.

DAUPHIN
My most redoubted father,
It is most meet we arm us 'gainst the foe;
For peace itself should not so dull a kingdom,
Though war nor no known quarrel were in question,
But that defences, musters, preparations,
Should be maintain'd, assembled and collected,
As were a war in expectation.
Therefore, I say 'tis meet we all go forth
To view the sick and feeble parts of France:
And let us do it with no show of fear;
No, with no more than if we heard that England
Were busied with a Whitsun morris-dance:
For, my good liege, she is so idly king'd,
Her sceptre so fantastically borne
By a vain, giddy, shallow, humorous youth,
That fear attends her not.

CONSTABLE
O peace, Prince Dauphin!
You are too much mistaken in this king:
Question your grace the late ambassadors,

With what great state he heard their embassy,
How well supplied with noble counsellors,
How modest in exception, and withal
How terrible in constant resolution,
And you shall find his vanities forespent
Were but the outside of the Roman Brutus,
Covering discretion with a coat of folly;
As gardeners do with ordure hide those roots
That shall first spring and be most delicate.

DAUPHIN
Well, 'tis not so, my lord high constable;
But though we think it so, it is no matter:
In cases of defence 'tis best to weigh
The enemy more mighty than he seems:
So the proportions of defence are fill'd;
Which of a weak or niggardly projection
Doth, like a miser, spoil his coat with scanting
A little cloth.

KING OF FRANCE
Think we King Harry strong;
And, princes, look you strongly arm to meet him.
The kindred of him hath been flesh'd upon us;
And he is bred out of that bloody strain
That haunted us in our familiar paths:
Witness our too much memorable shame
When Cressy battle fatally was struck,
And all our princes captiv'd by the hand
Of that black name, Edward, Black Prince of Wales;
Whiles that his mountain sire, on mountain standing,
Up in the air, crown'd with the golden sun,
Saw his heroical seed, and smiled to see him,
Mangle the work of nature and deface
The patterns that by God and by French fathers
Had twenty years been made. This is a stem
Of that victorious stock; and let us fear
The native mightiness and fate of him.

Enter a MESSENGER

MESSENGER
Ambassadors from Harry King of England
Do crave admittance to your majesty.

KING OF FRANCE
We'll give them present audience. Go, and bring them.

Exeunt MESSENGER and certain Lords

You see this chase is hotly follow'd, friends.

DAUPHIN
Turn head, and stop pursuit; for coward dogs
Most spend their mouths when what they seem to threaten
Runs far before them. Good my sovereign,
Take up the English short, and let them know
Of what a monarchy you are the head:
Self-love, my liege, is not so vile a sin
As self-neglecting.

Re-enter Lords, with EXETER and train

KING OF FRANCE
From our brother England?

EXETER
From him; and thus he greets your majesty.
He wills you, in the name of God Almighty,
That you divest yourself, and lay apart
The borrow'd glories that by gift of heaven,
By law of nature and of nations, 'long
To him and to his heirs; namely, the crown
And all wide-stretched honours that pertain
By custom and the ordinance of times
Unto the crown of France. That you may know
'Tis no sinister nor no awkward claim,
Pick'd from the worm-holes of long-vanish'd days,
Nor from the dust of old oblivion raked,
He sends you this most memorable line,
In every branch truly demonstrative;
Willing to overlook this pedigree:
And when you find him evenly derived
From his most famed of famous ancestors,
Edward the Third, he bids you then resign
Your crown and kingdom, indirectly held
From him the native and true challenger.

KING OF FRANCE
Or else what follows?

EXETER
Bloody constraint; for if you hide the crown
Even in your hearts, there will he rake for it:
Therefore in fierce tempest is he coming,
In thunder and in earthquake, like a Jove,
That, if requiring fail, he will compel;
And bids you, in the bowels of the Lord,
Deliver up the crown, and to take mercy
On the poor souls for whom this hungry war
Opens his vasty jaws; and on your head
Turning the widows' tears, the orphans' cries

The dead men's blood, the pining maidens groans,
For husbands, fathers and betrothed lovers,
That shall be swallow'd in this controversy.
This is his claim, his threatening and my message;
Unless the Dauphin be in presence here,
To whom expressly I bring greeting too.

KING OF FRANCE
For us, we will consider of this further:
To-morrow shall you bear our full intent
Back to our brother England.

DAUPHIN
For the Dauphin,
I stand here for him: what to him from England?

EXETER
Scorn and defiance; slight regard, contempt,
And any thing that may not misbecome
The mighty sender, doth he prize you at.
Thus says my king; an' if your father's highness
Do not, in grant of all demands at large,
Sweeten the bitter mock you sent his majesty,
He'll call you to so hot an answer of it,
That caves and womby vaultages of France
Shall chide your trespass and return your mock
In second accent of his ordnance.

DAUPHIN
Say, if my father render fair return,
It is against my will; for I desire
Nothing but odds with England: to that end,
As matching to his youth and vanity,
I did present him with the Paris balls.

EXETER
He'll make your Paris Louvre shake for it,
Were it the mistress-court of mighty Europe:
And, be assured, you'll find a difference,
As we his subjects have in wonder found,
Between the promise of his greener days
And these he masters now: now he weighs time
Even to the utmost grain: that you shall read
In your own losses, if he stay in France.

KING OF FRANCE
To-morrow shall you know our mind at full.

EXETER

Dispatch us with all speed, lest that our king
Come here himself to question our delay;
For he is footed in this land already.

KING OF FRANCE
You shall be soon dispatch's with fair conditions:
A night is but small breath and little pause
To answer matters of this consequence.

Flourish.

Exeunt

ACT III

PROLOGUE

Enter CHORUS

CHORUS
Thus with imagined wing our swift scene flies
In motion of no less celerity
Than that of thought. Suppose that you have seen
The well-appointed king at Hampton pier
Embark his royalty; and his brave fleet
With silken streamers the young Phoebus fanning:
Play with your fancies, and in them behold
Upon the hempen tackle ship-boys climbing;
Hear the shrill whistle which doth order give
To sounds confused; behold the threaden sails,
Borne with the invisible and creeping wind,
Draw the huge bottoms through the furrow'd sea,
Breasting the lofty surge: O, do but think
You stand upon the ravage and behold
A city on the inconstant billows dancing;
For so appears this fleet majestical,
Holding due course to Harfleur. Follow, follow:
Grapple your minds to sternage of this navy,
And leave your England, as dead midnight still,
Guarded with grandsires, babies and old women,
Either past or not arrived to pith and puissance;
For who is he, whose chin is but enrich'd
With one appearing hair, that will not follow
These cull'd and choice-drawn cavaliers to France?
Work, work your thoughts, and therein see a siege;
Behold the ordnance on their carriages,
With fatal mouths gaping on girded Harfleur.
Suppose the ambassador from the French comes back;

Tells Harry that the king doth offer him
Katharine his daughter, and with her, to dowry,
Some petty and unprofitable dukedoms.
The offer likes not: and the nimble gunner
With linstock now the devilish cannon touches,
Alarum, and chambers go off
And down goes all before them. Still be kind,
And eke out our performance with your mind.

Exit

SCENE I. France. Before Harfleur

Alarum.

Enter KING HENRY, EXETER, BEDFORD, GLOUCESTER, and Soldiers, with scaling-ladders

KING HENRY V
Once more unto the breach, dear friends, once more;
Or close the wall up with our English dead.
In peace there's nothing so becomes a man
As modest stillness and humility:
But when the blast of war blows in our ears,
Then imitate the action of the tiger;
Stiffen the sinews, summon up the blood,
Disguise fair nature with hard-favour'd rage;
Then lend the eye a terrible aspect;
Let pry through the portage of the head
Like the brass cannon; let the brow o'erwhelm it
As fearfully as doth a galled rock
O'erhang and jutty his confounded base,
Swill'd with the wild and wasteful ocean.
Now set the teeth and stretch the nostril wide,
Hold hard the breath and bend up every spirit
To his full height. On, on, you noblest English.
Whose blood is fet from fathers of war-proof!
Fathers that, like so many Alexanders,
Have in these parts from morn till even fought
And sheathed their swords for lack of argument:
Dishonour not your mothers; now attest
That those whom you call'd fathers did beget you.
Be copy now to men of grosser blood,
And teach them how to war. And you, good yeoman,
Whose limbs were made in England, show us here
The mettle of your pasture; let us swear
That you are worth your breeding; which I doubt not;
For there is none of you so mean and base,
That hath not noble lustre in your eyes.
I see you stand like greyhounds in the slips,

Straining upon the start. The game's afoot:
Follow your spirit, and upon this charge
Cry 'God for Harry, England, and Saint George!'

Exeunt. Alarum, and chambers go off

SCENE II. The Same

Enter NYM, BARDOLPH, PISTOL, and Boy

BARDOLPH
On, on, on, on, on! to the breach, to the breach!

NYM
Pray thee, corporal, stay: the knocks are too hot; and, for mine own part, I have not a case of lives: the humour of it is too hot, that is the very plain-song of it.

PISTOL
The plain-song is most just: for humours do abound:
Knocks go and come; God's vassals drop and die;
And sword and shield,
In bloody field,
Doth win immortal fame.

BOY
Would I were in an alehouse in London! I would give all my fame for a pot of ale and safety.

PISTOL
And I:
If wishes would prevail with me,
My purpose should not fail with me,
But thither would I hie.

BOY
As duly, but not as truly,
As bird doth sing on bough.

Enter FLUELLEN

FLUELLEN
Up to the breach, you dogs! avaunt, you cullions!

Driving them forward

PISTOL
Be merciful, great duke, to men of mould.
Abate thy rage, abate thy manly rage,
Abate thy rage, great duke!
Good bawcock, bate thy rage; use lenity, sweet chuck!

NYM
These be good humours! your honour wins bad humours.

Exeunt all but BOY

BOY
As young as I am, I have observed these three swashers. I am boy to them all three: but all they three, though they would serve me, could not be man to me; for indeed three such antics do not amount to a man. For Bardolph, he is white-livered and red-faced; by the means whereof a' faces it out, but fights not. For Pistol, he hath a killing tongue and a quiet sword; by the means whereof a' breaks words, and keeps whole weapons. For Nym, he hath heard that men of few words are the best men; and therefore he scorns to say his prayers, lest a' should be thought a coward: but his few bad words are matched with as few good deeds; for a' never broke any man's head but his own, and that was against a post when he was drunk. They will steal any thing, and call it purchase. Bardolph stole a lute-case, bore it twelve leagues, and sold it for three half pence. Nym and Bardolph are sworn brothers in filching, and in Calais they stole a fire-shovel: I knew by that piece of service the men would carry coals. They would have me as familiar with men's pockets as their gloves or their handkerchers: which makes much against my manhood, if I should take from another's pocket to put into mine; for it is plain pocketing up of wrongs. I must leave them, and seek some better service: their villany goes against my weak stomach, and therefore I must cast it up.

Exit

Re-enter FLUELLEN, GOWER following

GOWER
Captain Fluellen, you must come presently to the mines; the Duke of Gloucester would speak with you.

FLUELLEN
To the mines! tell you the duke, it is not so good to come to the mines; for, look you, the mines is not according to the disciplines of the war: the concavities of it is not sufficient; for, look you, the athversary, you may discuss unto the duke, look you, is digt himself four yard under the countermines: by Cheshu, I think a' will plough up all, if there is not better directions.

GOWER
The Duke of Gloucester, to whom the order of the siege is given, is altogether directed by an Irishman, a very valiant gentleman, i' faith.

FLUELLEN
It is Captain Macmorris, is it not?

GOWER
I think it be.

FLUELLEN
By Cheshu, he is an ass, as in the world: I will verify as much in his beard: be has no more directions in the true disciplines of the wars, look you, of the Roman disciplines, than is a puppy-dog.

Enter MACMORRIS and Captain JAMY

GOWER
Here a' comes; and the Scots captain, Captain Jamy, with him.

FLUELLEN
Captain Jamy is a marvellous falourous gentleman, that is certain; and of great expedition and knowledge in th' aunchient wars, upon my particular knowledge of his directions: by Cheshu, he will maintain his argument as well as any military man in the world, in the disciplines of the pristine wars of the Romans.

JAMY
I say gud-day, Captain Fluellen.

FLUELLEN
God-den to your worship, good Captain James.

GOWER
How now, Captain Macmorris! have you quit the mines? have the pioneers given o'er?

MACMORRIS
By Chrish, la! tish ill done: the work ish give over, the trompet sound the retreat. By my hand, I swear, and my father's soul, the work ish ill done; it ish give over: I would have blowed up the town, so Chrish save me, la! in an hour: O, tish ill done, tish ill done; by my hand, tish ill done!

FLUELLEN
Captain Macmorris, I beseech you now, will you voutsafe me, look you, a few disputations with you, as partly touching or concerning the disciplines of the war, the Roman wars, in the way of argument, look you, and friendly communication; partly to satisfy my opinion, and partly for the satisfaction, look you, of my mind, as touching the direction of the military discipline; that is the point.

JAMY
It sall be vary gud, gud feith, gud captains bath: and I sall quit you with gud leve, as I may pick occasion; that sall I, marry.

MACMORRIS
It is no time to discourse, so Chrish save me: the day is hot, and the weather, and the wars, and the king, and the dukes: it is no time to discourse. The town is beseeched, and the trumpet call us to the breach; and we talk, and, be Chrish, do nothing: 'tis shame for us all: so God sa' me, 'tis shame to stand still; it is shame, by my hand: and there is throats to be cut, and works to be done; and there ish nothing done, so Chrish sa' me, la!

JAMY
By the mess, ere theise eyes of mine take themselves to slomber, ay'll de gud service, or ay'll lig i' the grund for it; ay, or go to death; and ay'll pay 't as valourously as I may, that sall I suerly do, that is the breff and the long. Marry, I wad full fain hear some question 'tween you tway.

FLUELLEN
Captain Macmorris, I think, look you, under your correction, there is not many of your nation—

MACMORRIS

Of my nation! What ish my nation? Ish a villain, and a bastard, and a knave, and a rascal. What ish my nation? Who talks of my nation?

FLUELLEN
Look you, if you take the matter otherwise than is meant, Captain Macmorris, peradventure I shall think you do not use me with that affability as in discretion you ought to use me, look you: being as good a man as yourself, both in the disciplines of war, and in the derivation of my birth, and in other particularities.

MACMORRIS
I do not know you so good a man as myself: so Chrish save me, I will cut off your head.

GOWER
Gentlemen both, you will mistake each other.

JAMY
A! that's a foul fault.

A parley sounded

GOWER
The town sounds a parley.

FLUELLEN
Captain Macmorris, when there is more better opportunity to be required, look you, I will be so bold as to tell you I know the disciplines of war; and there is an end.

Exeunt

SCENE III. The Same. Before the Gates

The GOVERNOR and some Citizens on the walls; the English forces below.

Enter KING HENRY and his train

KING HENRY V
How yet resolves the governor of the town?
This is the latest parle we will admit;
Therefore to our best mercy give yourselves;
Or like to men proud of destruction
Defy us to our worst: for, as I am a soldier,
A name that in my thoughts becomes me best,
If I begin the battery once again,
I will not leave the half-achieved Harfleur
Till in her ashes she lie buried.
The gates of mercy shall be all shut up,
And the flesh'd soldier, rough and hard of heart,
In liberty of bloody hand shall range
With conscience wide as hell, mowing like grass

Your fresh-fair virgins and your flowering infants.
What is it then to me, if impious war,
Array'd in flames like to the prince of fiends,
Do, with his smirch'd complexion, all fell feats
Enlink'd to waste and desolation?
What is't to me, when you yourselves are cause,
If your pure maidens fall into the hand
Of hot and forcing violation?
What rein can hold licentious wickedness
When down the hill he holds his fierce career?
We may as bootless spend our vain command
Upon the enraged soldiers in their spoil
As send precepts to the leviathan
To come ashore. Therefore, you men of Harfleur,
Take pity of your town and of your people,
Whiles yet my soldiers are in my command;
Whiles yet the cool and temperate wind of grace
O'erblows the filthy and contagious clouds
Of heady murder, spoil and villany.
If not, why, in a moment look to see
The blind and bloody soldier with foul hand
Defile the locks of your shrill-shrieking daughters;
Your fathers taken by the silver beards,
And their most reverend heads dash'd to the walls,
Your naked infants spitted upon pikes,
Whiles the mad mothers with their howls confused
Do break the clouds, as did the wives of Jewry
At Herod's bloody-hunting slaughtermen.
What say you? will you yield, and this avoid,
Or, guilty in defence, be thus destroy'd?

GOVERNOR
Our expectation hath this day an end:
The Dauphin, whom of succors we entreated,
Returns us that his powers are yet not ready
To raise so great a siege. Therefore, great king,
We yield our town and lives to thy soft mercy.
Enter our gates; dispose of us and ours;
For we no longer are defensible.

KING HENRY V
Open your gates. Come, uncle Exeter,
Go you and enter Harfleur; there remain,
And fortify it strongly 'gainst the French:
Use mercy to them all. For us, dear uncle,
The winter coming on and sickness growing
Upon our soldiers, we will retire to Calais.
To-night in Harfleur we will be your guest;
To-morrow for the march are we addrest.

Flourish. The KING and his train enter the town

SCENE IV. The French King's Palace

Enter KATHARINE and ALICE

KATHARINE
Alice, tu as ete en Angleterre, et tu parles bien le langage.

ALICE
Un peu, madame.

KATHARINE
Je te prie, m'enseignez: il faut que j'apprenne a parler. Comment appelez-vous la main en Anglois?

ALICE
La main? elle est appelee de hand.

KATHARINE
De hand. Et les doigts?

ALICE
Les doigts? ma foi, j'oublie les doigts; mais je me souviendrai. Les doigts? je pense qu'ils sont appeles de fingres; oui, de fingres.

KATHARINE
La main, de hand; les doigts, de fingres. Je pense que je suis le bon ecolier; j'ai gagne deux mots d'Anglois vitement. Comment appelez-vous les ongles?

ALICE
Les ongles? nous les appelons de nails.

KATHARINE
De nails. Ecoutez; dites-moi, si je parle bien: de hand, de fingres, et de nails.

ALICE
C'est bien dit, madame; il est fort bon Anglois.

KATHARINE
Dites-moi l'Anglois pour le bras.

ALICE
De arm, madame.

KATHARINE
Et le coude?

ALICE
De elbow.

KATHARINE
De elbow. Je m'en fais la repetition de tous les mots que vous m'avez appris des a present.

ALICE
Il est trop difficile, madame, comme je pense.

KATHARINE
Excusez-moi, Alice; ecoutez: de hand, de fingres, de nails, de arma, de bilbow.

ALICE
De elbow, madame.

KATHARINE
O Seigneur Dieu, je m'en oublie! de elbow. Comment appelez-vous le col?

ALICE
De neck, madame.

KATHARINE
De nick. Et le menton?

ALICE
De chin.

KATHARINE
De sin. Le col, de nick; de menton, de sin.

ALICE
Oui. Sauf votre honneur, en verite, vous prononcez les mots aussi droit que les natifs d'Angleterre.

KATHARINE
Je ne doute point d'apprendre, par la grace de Dieu, et en peu de temps.

ALICE
N'avez vous pas deja oublie ce que je vous ai enseigne?

KATHARINE
Non, je reciterai a vous promptement: de hand, de fingres, de mails—

ALICE
De nails, madame.

KATHARINE
De nails, de arm, de ilbow.

ALICE
Sauf votre honneur, de elbow.

KATHARINE
Ainsi dis-je; de elbow, de nick, et de sin. Comment appelez-vous le pied et la robe?

ALICE
De foot, madame; et de coun.

KATHARINE
De foot et de coun! O Seigneur Dieu! ce sont mots de son mauvais, corruptible, gros, et impudique, et non pour les dames d'honneur d'user: je ne voudrais prononcer ces mots devant les seigneurs de France pour tout le monde. Foh! le foot et le coun! Neanmoins, je reciterai une autre fois ma lecon ensemble: de hand, de fingres, de nails, de arm, de elbow, de nick, de sin, de foot, de coun.

ALICE
Excellent, madame!

KATHARINE
C'est assez pour une fois: allons-nous a diner.

Exeunt

SCENE V. The Same

Enter the KING OF FRANCE, the DAUPHIN, the DUKE of BOURBON, the CONSTABLE of France, and others

KING OF FRANCE
'Tis certain he hath pass'd the river Somme.

CONSTABLE
And if he be not fought withal, my lord,
Let us not live in France; let us quit all
And give our vineyards to a barbarous people.

DAUPHIN
O Dieu vivant! shall a few sprays of us,
The emptying of our fathers' luxury,
Our scions, put in wild and savage stock,
Spirt up so suddenly into the clouds,
And overlook their grafters?

BOURBON
Normans, but bastard Normans, Norman bastards!
Mort de ma vie! if they march along
Unfought withal, but I will sell my dukedom,
To buy a slobbery and a dirty farm
In that nook-shotten isle of Albion.

CONSTABLE
Dieu de batailles! where have they this mettle?
Is not their climate foggy, raw and dull,
On whom, as in despite, the sun looks pale,
Killing their fruit with frowns? Can sodden water,

A drench for sur-rein'd jades, their barley-broth,
Decoct their cold blood to such valiant heat?
And shall our quick blood, spirited with wine,
Seem frosty? O, for honour of our land,
Let us not hang like roping icicles
Upon our houses' thatch, whiles a more frosty people
Sweat drops of gallant youth in our rich fields!
Poor we may call them in their native lords.

DAUPHIN
By faith and honour,
Our madams mock at us, and plainly say
Our mettle is bred out and they will give
Their bodies to the lust of English youth
To new-store France with bastard warriors.

BOURBON
They bid us to the English dancing-schools,
And teach lavoltas high and swift corantos;
Saying our grace is only in our heels,
And that we are most lofty runaways.

KING OF FRANCE
Where is Montjoy the herald? speed him hence:
Let him greet England with our sharp defiance.
Up, princes! and, with spirit of honour edged
More sharper than your swords, hie to the field:
Charles Delabreth, high constable of France;
You Dukes of Orleans, Bourbon, and of Berri,
Alencon, Brabant, Bar, and Burgundy;
Jaques Chatillon, Rambures, Vaudemont,
Beaumont, Grandpre, Roussi, and Fauconberg,
Foix, Lestrale, Bouciqualt, and Charolois;
High dukes, great princes, barons, lords and knights,
For your great seats now quit you of great shames.
Bar Harry England, that sweeps through our land
With pennons painted in the blood of Harfleur:
Rush on his host, as doth the melted snow
Upon the valleys, whose low vassal seat
The Alps doth spit and void his rheum upon:
Go down upon him, you have power enough,
And in a captive chariot into Rouen
Bring him our prisoner.

CONSTABLE
This becomes the great.
Sorry am I his numbers are so few,
His soldiers sick and famish'd in their march,
For I am sure, when he shall see our army,
He'll drop his heart into the sink of fear
And for achievement offer us his ransom.

KING OF FRANCE
Therefore, lord constable, haste on Montjoy.
And let him say to England that we send
To know what willing ransom he will give.
Prince Dauphin, you shall stay with us in Rouen.

DAUPHIN
Not so, I do beseech your majesty.

KING OF FRANCE
Be patient, for you shall remain with us.
Now forth, lord constable and princes all,
And quickly bring us word of England's fall.

Exeunt

SCENE VI. The English Camp in Picardy.

Enter GOWER and FLUELLEN, meeting

GOWER
How now, Captain Fluellen! come you from the bridge?

FLUELLEN
I assure you, there is very excellent services committed at the bridge.

GOWER
Is the Duke of Exeter safe?

FLUELLEN
The Duke of Exeter is as magnanimous as Agamemnon; and a man that I love and honour with my soul, and my heart, and my duty, and my life, and my living, and my uttermost power: he is not-God be praised and blessed!—any hurt in the world; but keeps the bridge most valiantly, with excellent discipline. There is an aunchient lieutenant there at the pridge, I think in my very conscience he is as valiant a man as Mark Antony; and he is a man of no estimation in the world; but did see him do as gallant service.

GOWER
What do you call him?

FLUELLEN
He is called Aunchient Pistol.

GOWER
I know him not.

Enter PISTOL

FLUELLEN
Here is the man.

PISTOL
Captain, I thee beseech to do me favours:
The Duke of Exeter doth love thee well.

FLUELLEN
Ay, I praise God; and I have merited some love at his hands.

PISTOL
Bardolph, a soldier, firm and sound of heart,
And of buxom valour, hath, by cruel fate,
And giddy Fortune's furious fickle wheel,
That goddess blind,
That stands upon the rolling restless stone—

FLUELLEN
By your patience, Aunchient Pistol. Fortune is painted blind, with a muffler afore her eyes, to signify to you that Fortune is blind; and she is painted also with a wheel, to signify to you, which is the moral of it, that she is turning, and inconstant, and mutability, and variation: and her foot, look you, is fixed upon a spherical stone, which rolls, and rolls, and rolls: in good truth, the poet makes a most excellent description of it: Fortune is an excellent moral.

PISTOL
Fortune is Bardolph's foe, and frowns on him;
For he hath stolen a pax, and hanged must a' be:
A damned death!
Let gallows gape for dog; let man go free
And let not hemp his wind-pipe suffocate:
But Exeter hath given the doom of death
For pax of little price.
Therefore, go speak: the duke will hear thy voice:
And let not Bardolph's vital thread be cut
With edge of penny cord and vile reproach:
Speak, captain, for his life, and I will thee requite.

FLUELLEN
Aunchient Pistol, I do partly understand your meaning.

PISTOL
Why then, rejoice therefore.

FLUELLEN
Certainly, aunchient, it is not a thing to rejoice at: for if, look you, he were my brother, I would desire the duke to use his good pleasure, and put him to execution; for discipline ought to be used.

PISTOL
Die and be damn'd! and figo for thy friendship!

FLUELLEN

It is well.

PISTOL
The fig of Spain!

Exit

FLUELLEN
Very good.

GOWER
Why, this is an arrant counterfeit rascal; I remember him now; a bawd, a cutpurse.

FLUELLEN
I'll assure you, a' uttered as brave words at the bridge as you shall see in a summer's day. But it is very well; what he has spoke to me, that is well, I warrant you, when time is serve.

GOWER
Why, 'tis a gull, a fool, a rogue, that now and then goes to the wars, to grace himself at his return into London under the form of a soldier. And such fellows are perfect in the great commanders' names: and they will learn you by rote where services were done; at such and such a sconce, at such a breach, at such a convoy; who came off bravely, who was shot, who disgraced, what terms the enemy stood on; and this they con perfectly in the phrase of war, which they trick up with new-tuned oaths: and what a beard of the general's cut and a horrid suit of the camp will do among foaming bottles and ale-washed wits, is wonderful to be thought on. But you must learn to know such slanders of the age, or else you may be marvellously mistook.

FLUELLEN
I tell you what, Captain Gower; I do perceive he is not the man that he would gladly make show to the world he is: if I find a hole in his coat, I will tell him my mind.

Drum heard

Hark you, the king is coming, and I must speak with him from the pridge.

Drum and colours.

Enter KING HENRY, GLOUCESTER, and Soldiers

God bless your majesty!

KING HENRY V
How now, Fluellen! camest thou from the bridge?

FLUELLEN
Ay, so please your majesty. The Duke of Exeter has very gallantly maintained the pridge: the French is gone off, look you; and there is gallant and most prave passages; marry, th' athversary was have possession of the pridge; but he is enforced to retire, and the Duke of Exeter is master of the pridge: I can tell your majesty, the duke is a prave man.

KING HENRY V

What men have you lost, Fluellen?

FLUELLEN
The perdition of th' athversary hath been very great, reasonable great: marry, for my part, I think the duke hath lost never a man, but one that is like to be executed for robbing a church, one Bardolph, if your majesty know the man: his face is all bubukles, and whelks, and knobs, and flames o' fire: and his lips blows at his nose, and it is like a coal of fire, sometimes plue and sometimes red; but his nose is executed and his fire's out.

KING HENRY V
We would have all such offenders so cut off: and we give express charge, that in our marches through the country, there be nothing compelled from the villages, nothing taken but paid for, none of the French upbraided or abused in disdainful language; for when lenity and cruelty play for a kingdom, the gentler gamester is the soonest winner.

Tucket.

Enter MONTJOY

MONTJOY
You know me by my habit.

KING HENRY V
Well then I know thee: what shall I know of thee?

MONTJOY
My master's mind.

KING HENRY V
Unfold it.

MONTJOY
Thus says my king: Say thou to Harry of England: Though we seemed dead, we did but sleep: advantage is a better soldier than rashness. Tell him we could have rebuked him at Harfleur, but that we thought not good to bruise an injury till it were full ripe: now we speak upon our cue, and our voice is imperial: England shall repent his folly, see his weakness, and admire our sufferance. Bid him therefore consider of his ransom; which must proportion the losses we have borne, the subjects we have lost, the disgrace we have digested; which in weight to re-answer, his pettiness would bow under. For our losses, his exchequer is too poor; for the effusion of our blood, the muster of his kingdom too faint a number; and for our disgrace, his own person, kneeling at our feet, but a weak and worthless satisfaction. To this add defiance: and tell him, for conclusion, he hath betrayed his followers, whose condemnation is pronounced. So far my king and master; so much my office.

KING HENRY V
What is thy name? I know thy quality.

MONTJOY
Montjoy.

KING HENRY V

Thou dost thy office fairly. Turn thee back.
And tell thy king I do not seek him now;
But could be willing to march on to Calais
Without impeachment: for, to say the sooth,
Though 'tis no wisdom to confess so much
Unto an enemy of craft and vantage,
My people are with sickness much enfeebled,
My numbers lessened, and those few I have
Almost no better than so many French;
Who when they were in health, I tell thee, herald,
I thought upon one pair of English legs
Did march three Frenchmen. Yet, forgive me, God,
That I do brag thus! This your air of France
Hath blown that vice in me: I must repent.
Go therefore, tell thy master here I am;
My ransom is this frail and worthless trunk,
My army but a weak and sickly guard;
Yet, God before, tell him we will come on,
Though France himself and such another neighbour
Stand in our way. There's for thy labour, Montjoy.
Go bid thy master well advise himself:
If we may pass, we will; if we be hinder'd,
We shall your tawny ground with your red blood
Discolour: and so Montjoy, fare you well.
The sum of all our answer is but this:
We would not seek a battle, as we are;
Nor, as we are, we say we will not shun it:
So tell your master.

MONTJOY
I shall deliver so. Thanks to your highness.

Exit

GLOUCESTER
I hope they will not come upon us now.

KING HENRY V
We are in God's hand, brother, not in theirs.
March to the bridge; it now draws toward night:
Beyond the river we'll encamp ourselves,
And on to-morrow, bid them march away.

Exeunt

SCENE VII. The French Camp, Near Agincourt:

Enter the CONSTABLE of France, the LORD RAMBURES, ORLEANS, DAUPHIN, with others

CONSTABLE
Tut! I have the best armour of the world. Would it were day!

ORLEANS
You have an excellent armour; but let my horse have his due.

CONSTABLE
It is the best horse of Europe.

ORLEANS
Will it never be morning?

DAUPHIN
My lord of Orleans, and my lord high constable, you
talk of horse and armour?

ORLEANS
You are as well provided of both as any prince in the world.

DAUPHIN
What a long night is this! I will not change my horse with any that treads but on four pasterns. Ca, ha! he bounds from the earth, as if his entrails were hairs; le cheval volant, the Pegasus, chez les narines de feu! When I bestride him, I soar, I am a hawk: he trots the air; the earth sings when he touches it; the basest horn of his hoof is more musical than the pipe of Hermes.

ORLEANS
He's of the colour of the nutmeg.

DAUPHIN
And of the heat of the ginger. It is a beast for Perseus: he is pure air and fire; and the dull elements of earth and water never appear in him, but only in Patient stillness while his rider mounts him: he is indeed a horse; and all other jades you may call beasts.

CONSTABLE
Indeed, my lord, it is a most absolute and excellent horse.

DAUPHIN
It is the prince of palfreys; his neigh is like the bidding of a monarch and his countenance enforces homage.

ORLEANS
No more, cousin.

DAUPHIN
Nay, the man hath no wit that cannot, from the rising of the lark to the lodging of the lamb, vary deserved praise on my palfrey: it is a theme as fluent as the sea: turn the sands into eloquent tongues, and my horse is argument for them all: 'tis a subject for a sovereign to reason on, and for a sovereign's sovereign to ride on; and for the world, familiar to us and unknown to lay apart their particular functions and wonder at him. I once writ a sonnet in his praise and began thus: 'Wonder of nature,'—

ORLEANS
I have heard a sonnet begin so to one's mistress.

DAUPHIN
Then did they imitate that which I composed to my courser, for my horse is my mistress.

ORLEANS
Your mistress bears well.

DAUPHIN
Me well; which is the prescript praise and perfection of a good and particular mistress.

Constable
Nay, for methought yesterday your mistress shrewdly shook your back.

DAUPHIN
So perhaps did yours.

Constable
Mine was not bridled.

DAUPHIN
O then belike she was old and gentle; and you rode, like a kern of Ireland, your French hose off, and in your straight strossers.

Constable
You have good judgment in horsemanship.

DAUPHIN
Be warned by me, then: they that ride so and ride not warily, fall into foul bogs. I had rather have my horse to my mistress.

Constable
I had as lief have my mistress a jade.

DAUPHIN
I tell thee, constable, my mistress wears his own hair.

CONSTABLE
I could make as true a boast as that, if I had a sow to my mistress.

DAUPHIN
'Le chien est retourne a son propre vomissement, et la truie lavee au bourbier;' thou makest use of any thing.

CONSTABLE
Yet do I not use my horse for my mistress, or any such proverb so little kin to the purpose.

RAMBURES
My lord constable, the armour that I saw in your tent to-night, are those stars or suns upon it?

CONSTABLE
Stars, my lord.

DAUPHIN
Some of them will fall to-morrow, I hope.

CONSTABLE
And yet my sky shall not want.

DAUPHIN
That may be, for you bear a many superfluously, and 'twere more honour some were away.

CONSTABLE
Even as your horse bears your praises; who would trot as well, were some of your brags dismounted.

DAUPHIN
Would I were able to load him with his desert! Will it never be day? I will trot to-morrow a mile, and my way shall be paved with English faces.

CONSTABLE
I will not say so, for fear I should be faced out of my way: but I would it were morning; for I would fain be about the ears of the English.

RAMBURES
Who will go to hazard with me for twenty prisoners?

CONSTABLE
You must first go yourself to hazard, ere you have them.

DAUPHIN
'Tis midnight; I'll go arm myself.

Exit

ORLEANS
The Dauphin longs for morning.

RAMBURES
He longs to eat the English.

CONSTABLE
I think he will eat all he kills.

ORLEANS
By the white hand of my lady, he's a gallant prince.

CONSTABLE
Swear by her foot, that she may tread out the oath.

ORLEANS
He is simply the most active gentleman of France.

CONSTABLE
Doing is activity; and he will still be doing.

ORLEANS
He never did harm, that I heard of.

CONSTABLE
Nor will do none to-morrow: he will keep that good name still.

ORLEANS
I know him to be valiant.

CONSTABLE
I was told that by one that knows him better than you.

ORLEANS
What's he?

CONSTABLE
Marry, he told me so himself; and he said he cared not who knew it

ORLEANS
He needs not; it is no hidden virtue in him.

CONSTABLE
By my faith, sir, but it is; never any body saw it but his lackey: 'tis a hooded valour; and when it appears, it will bate.

ORLEANS
Ill will never said well.

CONSTABLE
I will cap that proverb with 'There is flattery in friendship.'

ORLEANS
And I will take up that with 'Give the devil his due.'

CONSTABLE
Well placed: there stands your friend for the devil: have at the very eye of that proverb with 'A pox of the devil.'

ORLEANS
You are the better at proverbs, by how much 'A fool's bolt is soon shot.'

CONSTABLE
You have shot over.

ORLEANS
'Tis not the first time you were overshot.

Enter a MESSENGER

MESSENGER
My lord high constable, the English lie within fifteen hundred paces of your tents.

CONSTABLE
Who hath measured the ground?

MESSENGER
The Lord Grandpre.

CONSTABLE
A valiant and most expert gentleman. Would it were day! Alas, poor Harry of England! he longs not for the dawning as we do.

ORLEANS
What a wretched and peevish fellow is this king of England, to mope with his fat-brained followers so far out of his knowledge!

CONSTABLE
If the English had any apprehension, they would run away.

ORLEANS
That they lack; for if their heads had any intellectual armour, they could never wear such heavy head-pieces.

RAMBURES
That island of England breeds very valiant creatures; their mastiffs are of unmatchable courage.

ORLEANS
Foolish curs, that run winking into the mouth of a Russian bear and have their heads crushed like rotten apples! You may as well say, that's a valiant flea that dare eat his breakfast on the lip of a lion.

CONSTABLE
Just, just; and the men do sympathize with the mastiffs in robustious and rough coming on, leaving their wits with their wives: and then give them great meals of beef and iron and steel, they will eat like wolves and fight like devils.

ORLEANS
Ay, but these English are shrewdly out of beef.

CONSTABLE
Then shall we find to-morrow they have only stomachs to eat and none to fight. Now is it time to arm: come, shall we about it?

ORLEANS
It is now two o'clock: but, let me see, by ten
We shall have each a hundred Englishmen.

Exeunt

ACT IV

PROLOGUE

Enter CHORUS

CHORUS
Now entertain conjecture of a time
When creeping murmur and the poring dark
Fills the wide vessel of the universe.
From camp to camp through the foul womb of night
The hum of either army stilly sounds,
That the fixed sentinels almost receive
The secret whispers of each other's watch:
Fire answers fire, and through their paly flames
Each battle sees the other's umber'd face;
Steed threatens steed, in high and boastful neighs
Piercing the night's dull ear, and from the tents
The armourers, accomplishing the knights,
With busy hammers closing rivets up,
Give dreadful note of preparation:
The country cocks do crow, the clocks do toll,
And the third hour of drowsy morning name.
Proud of their numbers and secure in soul,
The confident and over-lusty French
Do the low-rated English play at dice;
And chide the cripple tardy-gaited night
Who, like a foul and ugly witch, doth limp
So tediously away. The poor condemned English,
Like sacrifices, by their watchful fires
Sit patiently and inly ruminate
The morning's danger, and their gesture sad
Investing lank-lean; cheeks and war-worn coats
Presenteth them unto the gazing moon
So many horrid ghosts. O now, who will behold
The royal captain of this ruin'd band
Walking from watch to watch, from tent to tent,
Let him cry 'Praise and glory on his head!'
For forth he goes and visits all his host.
Bids them good morrow with a modest smile
And calls them brothers, friends and countrymen.
Upon his royal face there is no note
How dread an army hath enrounded him;
Nor doth he dedicate one jot of colour
Unto the weary and all-watched night,
But freshly looks and over-bears attaint
With cheerful semblance and sweet majesty;
That every wretch, pining and pale before,

Beholding him, plucks comfort from his looks:
A largess universal like the sun
His liberal eye doth give to every one,
Thawing cold fear, that mean and gentle all,
Behold, as may unworthiness define,
A little touch of Harry in the night.
And so our scene must to the battle fly;
Where—O for pity!—we shall much disgrace
With four or five most vile and ragged foils,
Right ill-disposed in brawl ridiculous,
The name of Agincourt. Yet sit and see,
Minding true things by what their mockeries be.

Exit

SCENE I. The English Camp at Agincourt

Enter KING HENRY, BEDFORD, and GLOUCESTER

KING HENRY V
Gloucester, 'tis true that we are in great danger;
The greater therefore should our courage be.
Good morrow, brother Bedford. God Almighty!
There is some soul of goodness in things evil,
Would men observingly distil it out.
For our bad neighbour makes us early stirrers,
Which is both healthful and good husbandry:
Besides, they are our outward consciences,
And preachers to us all, admonishing
That we should dress us fairly for our end.
Thus may we gather honey from the weed,
And make a moral of the devil himself.

Enter ERPINGHAM

Good morrow, old Sir Thomas Erpingham:
A good soft pillow for that good white head
Were better than a churlish turf of France.

ERPINGHAM
Not so, my liege: this lodging likes me better,
Since I may say 'Now lie I like a king.'

KING HENRY V
'Tis good for men to love their present pains
Upon example; so the spirit is eased:
And when the mind is quicken'd, out of doubt,
The organs, though defunct and dead before,
Break up their drowsy grave and newly move,

With casted slough and fresh legerity.
Lend me thy cloak, Sir Thomas. Brothers both,
Commend me to the princes in our camp;
Do my good morrow to them, and anon
Desire them an to my pavilion.

GLOUCESTER
We shall, my liege.

ERPINGHAM
Shall I attend your grace?

KING HENRY V
No, my good knight;
Go with my brothers to my lords of England:
I and my bosom must debate awhile,
And then I would no other company.

ERPINGHAM
The Lord in heaven bless thee, noble Harry!

Exeunt all but KING HENRY

KING HENRY V
God-a-mercy, old heart! thou speak'st cheerfully.

Enter PISTOL

PISTOL
Qui va la?

KING HENRY V
A friend.

PISTOL
Discuss unto me; art thou officer?
Or art thou base, common and popular?

KING HENRY V
I am a gentleman of a company.

PISTOL
Trail'st thou the puissant pike?

KING HENRY V
Even so. What are you?

PISTOL
As good a gentleman as the emperor.

KING HENRY V

Then you are a better than the king.

PISTOL
The king's a bawcock, and a heart of gold,
A lad of life, an imp of fame;
Of parents good, of fist most valiant.
I kiss his dirty shoe, and from heart-string
I love the lovely bully. What is thy name?

KING HENRY V
Harry le Roy.

PISTOL
Le Roy! a Cornish name: art thou of Cornish crew?

KING HENRY V
No, I am a Welshman.

PISTOL
Know'st thou Fluellen?

KING HENRY V
Yes.

PISTOL
Tell him, I'll knock his leek about his pate
Upon Saint Davy's day.

KING HENRY V
Do not you wear your dagger in your cap that day, lest he knock that about yours.

PISTOL
Art thou his friend?

KING HENRY V
And his kinsman too.

PISTOL
The figo for thee, then!

KING HENRY V
I thank you: God be with you!

PISTOL
My name is Pistol call'd.

Exit

KING HENRY V
It sorts well with your fierceness.

Enter FLUELLEN and GOWER

GOWER
Captain Fluellen!

FLUELLEN
So! in the name of Jesu Christ, speak lower. It is the greatest admiration of the universal world, when the true and aunchient prerogatifes and laws of the wars is not kept: if you would take the pains but to examine the wars of Pompey the Great, you shall find, I warrant you, that there is no tiddle toddle nor pibble pabble in Pompey's camp; I warrant you, you shall find the ceremonies of the wars, and the cares of it, and the forms of it, and the sobriety of it, and the modesty of it, to be otherwise.

GOWER
Why, the enemy is loud; you hear him all night.

FLUELLEN
If the enemy is an ass and a fool and a prating coxcomb, is it meet, think you, that we should also, look you, be an ass and a fool and a prating coxcomb? in your own conscience, now?

GOWER
I will speak lower.

FLUELLEN
I pray you and beseech you that you will.

Exeunt GOWER and FLUELLEN

KING HENRY V
Though it appear a little out of fashion,
There is much care and valour in this Welshman.

Enter three soldiers, JOHN BATES, ALEXANDER COURT, and MICHAEL WILLIAMS

COURT
Brother John Bates, is not that the morning which breaks yonder?

BATES
I think it be: but we have no great cause to desire the approach of day.

WILLIAMS
We see yonder the beginning of the day, but I think we shall never see the end of it. Who goes there?

KING HENRY V
A friend.

WILLIAMS
Under what captain serve you?

KING HENRY V
Under Sir Thomas Erpingham.

WILLIAMS
A good old commander and a most kind gentleman: I pray you, what thinks he of our estate?

KING HENRY V
Even as men wrecked upon a sand, that look to be washed off the next tide.

BATES
He hath not told his thought to the king?

KING HENRY V
No; nor it is not meet he should. For, though I speak it to you, I think the king is but a man, as I am: the violet smells to him as it doth to me: the element shows to him as it doth to me; all his senses have but human conditions: his ceremonies laid by, in his nakedness he appears but a man; and though his affections are higher mounted than ours, yet, when they stoop, they stoop with the like wing. Therefore when he sees reason of fears, as we do, his fears, out of doubt, be of the same relish as ours are: yet, in reason, no man should possess him with any appearance of fear, lest he, by showing it, should dishearten his army.

BATES
He may show what outward courage he will; but I believe, as cold a night as 'tis, he could wish himself in Thames up to the neck; and so I would he were, and I by him, at all adventures, so we were quit here.

KING HENRY V
By my troth, I will speak my conscience of the king: I think he would not wish himself any where but where he is.

BATES
Then I would he were here alone; so should he be sure to be ransomed, and a many poor men's lives saved.

KING HENRY V
I dare say you love him not so ill, to wish him here alone, howsoever you speak this to feel other men's minds: methinks I could not die any where so contented as in the king's company; his cause being just and his quarrel honourable.

WILLIAMS
That's more than we know.

BATES
Ay, or more than we should seek after; for we know enough, if we know we are the kings subjects: if his cause be wrong, our obedience to the king wipes the crime of it out of us.

WILLIAMS
But if the cause be not good, the king himself hath a heavy reckoning to make, when all those legs and arms and heads, chopped off in battle, shall join together at the latter day and cry all 'We died at such a place;' some swearing, some crying for a surgeon, some upon their wives left poor behind them, some upon the debts they owe, some upon their children rawly left. I am afeard there are few die well that die in a battle; for how can they charitably dispose of any thing, when blood is their

argument? Now, if these men do not die well, it will be a black matter for the king that led them to it; whom to disobey were against all proportion of subjection.

KING HENRY V
So, if a son that is by his father sent about merchandise do sinfully miscarry upon the sea, the imputation of his wickedness by your rule, should be imposed upon his father that sent him: or if a servant, under his master's command transporting a sum of money, be assailed by robbers and die in many irreconciled iniquities, you may call the business of the master the author of the servant's damnation: but this is not so: the king is not bound to answer the particular endings of his soldiers, the father of his son, nor the master of his servant; for they purpose not their death, when they purpose their services. Besides, there is no king, be his cause never so spotless, if it come to the arbitrement of swords, can try it out with all unspotted soldiers: some peradventure have on them the guilt of premeditated and contrived murder; some, of beguiling virgins with the broken seals of perjury; some, making the wars their bulwark, that have before gored the gentle bosom of peace with pillage and robbery. Now, if these men have defeated the law and outrun native punishment, though they can outstrip men, they have no wings to fly from God: war is his beadle, war is vengeance; so that here men are punished for before-breach of the king's laws in now the king's quarrel: where they feared the death, they have borne life away; and where they would be safe, they perish: then if they die unprovided, no more is the king guilty of their damnation than he was before guilty of those impieties for the which they are now visited. Every subject's duty is the king's; but every subject's soul is his own. Therefore should every soldier in the wars do as every sick man in his bed, wash every mote out of his conscience: and dying so, death is to him advantage; or not dying, the time was blessedly lost wherein such preparation was gained: and in him that escapes, it were not sin to think that, making God so free an offer, He let him outlive that day to see His greatness and to teach others how they should prepare.

WILLIAMS
'Tis certain, every man that dies ill, the ill upon his own head, the king is not to answer it.

BATES
But I do not desire he should answer for me; and yet I determine to fight lustily for him.

KING HENRY V
I myself heard the king say he would not be ransomed.

WILLIAMS
Ay, he said so, to make us fight cheerfully: but when our throats are cut, he may be ransomed, and we ne'er the wiser.

KING HENRY V
If I live to see it, I will never trust his word after.

WILLIAMS
You pay him then. That's a perilous shot out of an elder-gun, that a poor and private displeasure can do against a monarch! you may as well go about to turn the sun to ice with fanning in his face with a peacock's feather. You'll never trust his word after! come, 'tis a foolish saying.

KING HENRY V
Your reproof is something too round: I should be angry with you, if the time were convenient.

WILLIAMS

Let it be a quarrel between us, if you live.

KING HENRY V
I embrace it.

WILLIAMS
How shall I know thee again?

KING HENRY V
Give me any gage of thine, and I will wear it in my bonnet: then, if ever thou darest acknowledge it, I will make it my quarrel.

WILLIAMS
Here's my glove: give me another of thine.

KING HENRY V
There.

WILLIAMS
This will I also wear in my cap: if ever thou come to me and say, after to-morrow, 'This is my glove,' by this hand, I will take thee a box on the ear.

KING HENRY V
If ever I live to see it, I will challenge it.

WILLIAMS
Thou darest as well be hanged.

KING HENRY V
Well. I will do it, though I take thee in the king's company.

WILLIAMS
Keep thy word: fare thee well.

BATES
Be friends, you English fools, be friends: we have French quarrels enow, if you could tell how to reckon.

KING HENRY V
Indeed, the French may lay twenty French crowns to
One, they will beat us; for they bear them on their
Shoulders: but it is no English treason to cut
French crowns, and to-morrow the king himself will
Be a clipper.

Exeunt Soldiers

Upon the king! let us our lives, our souls,
Our debts, our careful wives,
Our children and our sins lay on the king!
We must bear all. O hard condition,

Twin-born with greatness, subject to the breath
Of every fool, whose sense no more can feel
But his own wringing! What infinite heart's-ease
Must kings neglect, that private men enjoy!
And what have kings, that privates have not too,
Save ceremony, save general ceremony?
And what art thou, thou idle ceremony?
What kind of god art thou, that suffer'st more
Of mortal griefs than do thy worshippers?
What are thy rents? what are thy comings in?
O ceremony, show me but thy worth!
What is thy soul of adoration?
Art thou aught else but place, degree and form,
Creating awe and fear in other men?
Wherein thou art less happy being fear'd
Than they in fearing.
What drink'st thou oft, instead of homage sweet,
But poison'd flattery? O, be sick, great greatness,
And bid thy ceremony give thee cure!
Think'st thou the fiery fever will go out
With titles blown from adulation?
Will it give place to flexure and low bending?
Canst thou, when thou command'st the beggar's knee,
Command the health of it? No, thou proud dream,
That play'st so subtly with a king's repose;
I am a king that find thee, and I know
'Tis not the balm, the sceptre and the ball,
The sword, the mace, the crown imperial,
The intertissued robe of gold and pearl,
The farced title running 'fore the king,
The throne he sits on, nor the tide of pomp
That beats upon the high shore of this world,
No, not all these, thrice-gorgeous ceremony,
Not all these, laid in bed majestical,
Can sleep so soundly as the wretched slave,
Who with a body fill'd and vacant mind
Gets him to rest, cramm'd with distressful bread;
Never sees horrid night, the child of hell,
But, like a lackey, from the rise to set
Sweats in the eye of Phoebus and all night
Sleeps in Elysium; next day after dawn,
Doth rise and help Hyperion to his horse,
And follows so the ever-running year,
With profitable labour, to his grave:
And, but for ceremony, such a wretch,
Winding up days with toil and nights with sleep,
Had the fore-hand and vantage of a king.
The slave, a member of the country's peace,
Enjoys it; but in gross brain little wots
What watch the king keeps to maintain the peace,
Whose hours the peasant best advantages.

Enter ERPINGHAM

ERPINGHAM
My lord, your nobles, jealous of your absence,
Seek through your camp to find you.

KING HENRY V
Good old knight,
Collect them all together at my tent:
I'll be before thee.

ERPINGHAM
I shall do't, my lord.

Exit

KING HENRY V
O God of battles! steel my soldiers' hearts;
Possess them not with fear; take from them now
The sense of reckoning, if the opposed numbers
Pluck their hearts from them. Not to-day, O Lord,
O, not to-day, think not upon the fault
My father made in compassing the crown!
I Richard's body have interred anew;
And on it have bestow'd more contrite tears
Than from it issued forced drops of blood:
Five hundred poor I have in yearly pay,
Who twice a-day their wither'd hands hold up
Toward heaven, to pardon blood; and I have built
Two chantries, where the sad and solemn priests
Sing still for Richard's soul. More will I do;
Though all that I can do is nothing worth,
Since that my penitence comes after all,
Imploring pardon.

Enter GLOUCESTER

GLOUCESTER
My liege!

KING HENRY V
My brother Gloucester's voice? Ay;
I know thy errand, I will go with thee:
The day, my friends and all things stay for me.

Exeunt

SCENE II. The French Camp

Enter the DAUPHIN, ORLEANS, RAMBURES, and others

ORLEANS
The sun doth gild our armour; up, my lords!

DAUPHIN
Montez A cheval! My horse! varlet! laquais! ha!

ORLEANS
O brave spirit!

DAUPHIN
Via! les eaux et la terre.

ORLEANS
Rien puis? L'air et la feu.

DAUPHIN
Ciel, cousin Orleans.

Enter CONSTABLE

Now, my lord constable!

CONSTABLE
Hark, how our steeds for present service neigh!

DAUPHIN
Mount them, and make incision in their hides,
That their hot blood may spin in English eyes,
And dout them with superfluous courage, ha!

RAMBURES
What, will you have them weep our horses' blood?
How shall we, then, behold their natural tears?

Enter MESSENGER

MESSENGER
The English are embattled, you French peers.

CONSTABLE
To horse, you gallant princes! straight to horse!
Do but behold yon poor and starved band,
And your fair show shall suck away their souls,
Leaving them but the shales and husks of men.
There is not work enough for all our hands;
Scarce blood enough in all their sickly veins
To give each naked curtle-axe a stain,
That our French gallants shall to-day draw out,

And sheathe for lack of sport: let us but blow on them,
The vapour of our valour will o'erturn them.
'Tis positive 'gainst all exceptions, lords,
That our superfluous lackeys and our peasants,
Who in unnecessary action swarm
About our squares of battle, were enow
To purge this field of such a hilding foe,
Though we upon this mountain's basis by
Took stand for idle speculation:
But that our honours must not. What's to say?
A very little little let us do.
And all is done. Then let the trumpets sound
The tucket sonance and the note to mount;
For our approach shall so much dare the field
That England shall couch down in fear and yield.

Enter GRANDPRE

GRANDPRE
Why do you stay so long, my lords of France?
Yon island carrions, desperate of their bones,
Ill-favouredly become the morning field:
Their ragged curtains poorly are let loose,
And our air shakes them passing scornfully:
Big Mars seems bankrupt in their beggar'd host
And faintly through a rusty beaver peeps:
The horsemen sit like fixed candlesticks,
With torch-staves in their hand; and their poor jades
Lob down their heads, dropping the hides and hips,
The gum down-roping from their pale-dead eyes
And in their pale dull mouths the gimmal bit
Lies foul with chew'd grass, still and motionless;
And their executors, the knavish crows,
Fly o'er them, all impatient for their hour.
Description cannot suit itself in words
To demonstrate the life of such a battle
In life so lifeless as it shows itself.

CONSTABLE
They have said their prayers, and they stay for death.

DAUPHIN
Shall we go send them dinners and fresh suits
And give their fasting horses provender,
And after fight with them?

CONSTABLE
I stay but for my guidon: to the field!
I will the banner from a trumpet take,
And use it for my haste. Come, come, away!
The sun is high, and we outwear the day.

Exeunt

SCENE III. The English Camp

Enter GLOUCESTER, BEDFORD, EXETER, ERPINGHAM, with all his host: SALISBURY and WESTMORELAND

GLOUCESTER
Where is the king?

BEDFORD
The king himself is rode to view their battle.

WESTMORELAND
Of fighting men they have full three score thousand.

EXETER
There's five to one; besides, they all are fresh.

SALISBURY
God's arm strike with us! 'tis a fearful odds.
God be wi' you, princes all; I'll to my charge:
If we no more meet till we meet in heaven,
Then, joyfully, my noble Lord of Bedford,
My dear Lord Gloucester, and my good Lord Exeter,
And my kind kinsman, warriors all, adieu!

BEDFORD
Farewell, good Salisbury; and good luck go with thee!

EXETER
Farewell, kind lord; fight valiantly to-day:
And yet I do thee wrong to mind thee of it,
For thou art framed of the firm truth of valour.

Exit SALISBURY

BEDFORD
He is full of valour as of kindness;
Princely in both.

Enter the KING

WESTMORELAND
O that we now had here
But one ten thousand of those men in England
That do no work to-day!

KING HENRY V
What's he that wishes so?
My cousin Westmoreland? No, my fair cousin:
If we are mark'd to die, we are enow
To do our country loss; and if to live,
The fewer men, the greater share of honour.
God's will! I pray thee, wish not one man more.
By Jove, I am not covetous for gold,
Nor care I who doth feed upon my cost;
It yearns me not if men my garments wear;
Such outward things dwell not in my desires:
But if it be a sin to covet honour,
I am the most offending soul alive.
No, faith, my coz, wish not a man from England:
God's peace! I would not lose so great an honour
As one man more, methinks, would share from me
For the best hope I have. O, do not wish one more!
Rather proclaim it, Westmoreland, through my host,
That he which hath no stomach to this fight,
Let him depart; his passport shall be made
And crowns for convoy put into his purse:
We would not die in that man's company
That fears his fellowship to die with us.
This day is called the feast of Crispian:
He that outlives this day, and comes safe home,
Will stand a tip-toe when the day is named,
And rouse him at the name of Crispian.
He that shall live this day, and see old age,
Will yearly on the vigil feast his neighbours,
And say 'To-morrow is Saint Crispian:'
Then will he strip his sleeve and show his scars.
And say 'These wounds I had on Crispin's day.'
Old men forget: yet all shall be forgot,
But he'll remember with advantages
What feats he did that day: then shall our names.
Familiar in his mouth as household words
Harry the king, Bedford and Exeter,
Warwick and Talbot, Salisbury and Gloucester,
Be in their flowing cups freshly remember'd.
This story shall the good man teach his son;
And Crispin Crispian shall ne'er go by,
From this day to the ending of the world,
But we in it shall be remember'd;
We few, we happy few, we band of brothers;
For he to-day that sheds his blood with me
Shall be my brother; be he ne'er so vile,
This day shall gentle his condition:
And gentlemen in England now a-bed
Shall think themselves accursed they were not here,
And hold their manhoods cheap whiles any speaks
That fought with us upon Saint Crispin's day.

Re-enter SALISBURY

SALISBURY
My sovereign lord, bestow yourself with speed:
The French are bravely in their battles set,
And will with all expedience charge on us.

KING HENRY V
All things are ready, if our minds be so.

WESTMORELAND
Perish the man whose mind is backward now!

KING HENRY V
Thou dost not wish more help from England, coz?

WESTMORELAND
God's will! my liege, would you and I alone,
Without more help, could fight this royal battle!

KING HENRY V
Why, now thou hast unwish'd five thousand men;
Which likes me better than to wish us one.
You know your places: God be with you all!

Tucket. Enter MONTJOY

MONTJOY
Once more I come to know of thee, King Harry,
If for thy ransom thou wilt now compound,
Before thy most assured overthrow:
For certainly thou art so near the gulf,
Thou needs must be englutted. Besides, in mercy,
The constable desires thee thou wilt mind
Thy followers of repentance; that their souls
May make a peaceful and a sweet retire
From off these fields, where, wretches, their poor bodies
Must lie and fester.

KING HENRY V
Who hath sent thee now?

MONTJOY
The Constable of France.

KING HENRY V
I pray thee, bear my former answer back:
Bid them achieve me and then sell my bones.
Good God! why should they mock poor fellows thus?
The man that once did sell the lion's skin

While the beast lived, was killed with hunting him.
A many of our bodies shall no doubt
Find native graves; upon the which, I trust,
Shall witness live in brass of this day's work:
And those that leave their valiant bones in France,
Dying like men, though buried in your dunghills,
They shall be famed; for there the sun shall greet them,
And draw their honours reeking up to heaven;
Leaving their earthly parts to choke your clime,
The smell whereof shall breed a plague in France.
Mark then abounding valour in our English,
That being dead, like to the bullet's grazing,
Break out into a second course of mischief,
Killing in relapse of mortality.
Let me speak proudly: tell the constable
We are but warriors for the working-day;
Our gayness and our gilt are all besmirch'd
With rainy marching in the painful field;
There's not a piece of feather in our host—
Good argument, I hope, we will not fly—
And time hath worn us into slovenry:
But, by the mass, our hearts are in the trim;
And my poor soldiers tell me, yet ere night
They'll be in fresher robes, or they will pluck
The gay new coats o'er the French soldiers' heads
And turn them out of service. If they do this,—
As, if God please, they shall,—my ransom then
Will soon be levied. Herald, save thou thy labour;
Come thou no more for ransom, gentle herald:
They shall have none, I swear, but these my joints;
Which if they have as I will leave 'em them,
Shall yield them little, tell the constable.

MONTJOY
I shall, King Harry. And so fare thee well:
Thou never shalt hear herald any more.

Exit

KING HENRY V
I fear thou'lt once more come again for ransom.

Enter YORK

YORK
My lord, most humbly on my knee I beg
The leading of the vaward.

KING HENRY V
Take it, brave York. Now, soldiers, march away:
And how thou pleasest, God, dispose the day!

Exeunt

SCENE IV. The Field of Battle

Alarum. Excursions. Enter PISTOL, French Soldier, and Boy

PISTOL
Yield, cur!

FRENCH SOLDIER
Je pense que vous etes gentilhomme de bonne qualite.

PISTOL
Qualtitie calmie custure me! Art thou a gentleman?
What is thy name? discuss.

FRENCH SOLDIER
O Seigneur Dieu!

PISTOL
O, Signieur Dew should be a gentleman:
Perpend my words, O Signieur Dew, and mark;
O Signieur Dew, thou diest on point of fox,
Except, O signieur, thou do give to me
Egregious ransom.

FRENCH SOLDIER
O, prenez misericorde! ayez pitie de moi!

PISTOL
Moy shall not serve; I will have forty moys;
Or I will fetch thy rim out at thy throat
In drops of crimson blood.

FRENCH SOLDIER
Est-il impossible d'echapper la force de ton bras?

PISTOL
Brass, cur!
Thou damned and luxurious mountain goat,
Offer'st me brass?

FRENCH SOLDIER
O pardonnez moi!

PISTOL

Say'st thou me so? is that a ton of moys?
Come hither, boy: ask me this slave in French
What is his name.

BOY
Ecoutez: comment etes-vous appele?

FRENCH SOLDIER
Monsieur le Fer.

BOY
He says his name is Master Fer.

PISTOL
Master Fer! I'll fer him, and firk him, and ferret him: discuss the same in French unto him.

BOY
I do not know the French for fer, and ferret, and firk.

PISTOL
Bid him prepare; for I will cut his throat.

FRENCH SOLDIER
Que dit-il, monsieur?

BOY
Il me commande de vous dire que vous faites vous pret; car ce soldat ici est dispose tout a cette heure de couper votre gorge.

PISTOL
Owy, cuppele gorge, permafoy,
Peasant, unless thou give me crowns, brave crowns;
Or mangled shalt thou be by this my sword.

French Soldier
O, je vous supplie, pour l'amour de Dieu, me pardonner! Je suis gentilhomme de bonne maison: gardez ma vie, et je vous donnerai deux cents ecus.

PISTOL
What are his words?

BOY
He prays you to save his life: he is a gentleman of a good house; and for his ransom he will give you two hundred crowns.

PISTOL
Tell him my fury shall abate, and I the crowns will take.

FRENCH SOLDIER
Petit monsieur, que dit-il?

BOY
Encore qu'il est contre son jurement de pardoner aucun prisonnier, neanmoins, pour les ecus que vous l'avez promis, il est content de vous donner la liberte, le franchisement.

FRENCH SOLDIER
Sur mes genoux je vous donne mille remercimens; et je m'estime heureux que je suis tombe entre les mains d'un chevalier, je pense, le plus brave, vaillant, et tres distingue seigneur d'Angleterre.

PISTOL
Expound unto me, boy.

Boy
He gives you, upon his knees, a thousand thanks; and he esteems himself happy that he hath fallen into the hands of one, as he thinks, the most brave, valorous, and thrice-worthy signieur of England.

PISTOL
As I suck blood, I will some mercy show.
Follow me!

BOY
Suivez-vous le grand capitaine.

Exeunt PISTOL, and French SOLDIER

I did never know so full a voice issue from so empty a heart: but the saying is true 'The empty vessel makes the greatest sound.' Bardolph and Nym had ten times more valour than this roaring devil i' the old play, that every one may pare his nails with a wooden dagger; and they are both hanged; and so would this be, if he durst steal any thing adventurously. I must stay with the lackeys, with the luggage of our camp: the French might have a good prey of us, if he knew of it; for there is none to guard it but boys.

Exit

SCENE V. Another Part of the Field

Enter CONSTABLE, ORLEANS, BOURBON, DAUPHIN, and RAMBURES

CONSTABLE
O diable!

ORLEANS
O seigneur! le jour est perdu, tout est perdu!

DAUPHIN
Mort de ma vie! all is confounded, all!
Reproach and everlasting shame
Sits mocking in our plumes. O merchante fortune!
Do not run away.

A short alarum

CONSTABLE
Why, all our ranks are broke.

DAUPHIN
O perdurable shame! let's stab ourselves.
Be these the wretches that we play'd at dice for?

ORLEANS
Is this the king we sent to for his ransom?

BOURBON
Shame and eternal shame, nothing but shame!
Let us die in honour: once more back again;
And he that will not follow Bourbon now,
Let him go hence, and with his cap in hand,
Like a base pander, hold the chamber-door
Whilst by a slave, no gentler than my dog,
His fairest daughter is contaminated.

CONSTABLE
Disorder, that hath spoil'd us, friend us now!
Let us on heaps go offer up our lives.

ORLEANS
We are enow yet living in the field
To smother up the English in our throngs,
If any order might be thought upon.

BOURBON
The devil take order now! I'll to the throng:
Let life be short; else shame will be too long.

Exeunt

SCENE VI. Another Part of the Field.

Alarums.

Enter KING HENRY and forces, EXETER, and others

KING HENRY V
Well have we done, thrice valiant countrymen:
But all's not done; yet keep the French the field.

EXETER
The Duke of York commends him to your majesty.

KING HENRY V
Lives he, good uncle? thrice within this hour
I saw him down; thrice up again and fighting;
From helmet to the spur all blood he was.

EXETER
In which array, brave soldier, doth he lie,
Larding the plain; and by his bloody side,
Yoke-fellow to his honour-owing wounds,
The noble Earl of Suffolk also lies.
Suffolk first died: and York, all haggled over,
Comes to him, where in gore he lay insteep'd,
And takes him by the beard; kisses the gashes
That bloodily did spawn upon his face;
And cries aloud 'Tarry, dear cousin Suffolk!
My soul shall thine keep company to heaven;
Tarry, sweet soul, for mine, then fly abreast,
As in this glorious and well-foughten field
We kept together in our chivalry!'
Upon these words I came and cheer'd him up:
He smiled me in the face, raught me his hand,
And, with a feeble gripe, says 'Dear my lord,
Commend my service to me sovereign.'
So did he turn and over Suffolk's neck
He threw his wounded arm and kiss'd his lips;
And so espoused to death, with blood he seal'd
A testament of noble-ending love.
The pretty and sweet manner of it forced
Those waters from me which I would have stopp'd;
But I had not so much of man in me,
And all my mother came into mine eyes
And gave me up to tears.

KING HENRY V
I blame you not;
For, hearing this, I must perforce compound
With mistful eyes, or they will issue too.

Alarum

But, hark! what new alarum is this same?
The French have reinforced their scatter'd men:
Then every soldier kill his prisoners:
Give the word through.

Exeunt

SCENE VII. Another Part of the Field.

Enter FLUELLEN and GOWER

FLUELLEN
Kill the poys and the luggage! 'tis expressly against the law of arms: 'tis as arrant a piece of knavery, mark you now, as can be offer't; in your conscience, now, is it not?

GOWER
'Tis certain there's not a boy left alive; and the cowardly rascals that ran from the battle ha' done this slaughter: besides, they have burned and carried away all that was in the king's tent; wherefore the king, most worthily, hath caused every soldier to cut his prisoner's throat. O, 'tis a gallant king!

FLUELLEN
Ay, he was porn at Monmouth, Captain Gower. What call you the town's name where Alexander the Pig was born!

GOWER
Alexander the Great.

FLUELLEN
Why, I pray you, is not pig great? the pig, or the great, or the mighty, or the huge, or the magnanimous, are all one reckonings, save the phrase is a little variations.

GOWER
I think Alexander the Great was born in Macedon; his father was called Philip of Macedon, as I take it.

FLUELLEN
I think it is in Macedon where Alexander is porn. I tell you, captain, if you look in the maps of the 'orld, I warrant you sall find, in the comparisons between Macedon and Monmouth, that the situations, look you, is both alike. There is a river in Macedon; and there is also moreover a river at Monmouth: it is called Wye at Monmouth; but it is out of my prains what is the name of the other river; but 'tis all one, 'tis alike as my fingers is to my fingers, and there is salmons in both. If you mark Alexander's life well, Harry of Monmouth's life is come after it indifferent well; for there is figures in all things. Alexander, God knows, and you know, in his rages, and his furies, and his wraths, and his cholers, and his moods, and his displeasures, and his indignations, and also being a little intoxicates in his prains, did, in his ales and his angers, look you, kill his best friend, Cleitus.

GOWER
Our king is not like him in that: he never killed any of his friends.

FLUELLEN
It is not well done, mark you now take the tales out of my mouth, ere it is made and finished. I speak but in the figures and comparisons of it: as Alexander killed his friend Cleitus, being in his ales and his cups; so also Harry Monmouth, being in his right wits and his good judgments, turned away the fat knight with the great belly-doublet: he was full of jests, and gipes, and knaveries, and mocks; I have forgot his name.

GOWER
Sir John Falstaff.

FLUELLEN
That is he: I'll tell you there is good men porn at Monmouth.

GOWER
Here comes his majesty.

Alarum.

Enter KING HENRY, and forces; WARWICK, GLOUCESTER, EXETER, and others

KING HENRY V
I was not angry since I came to France
Until this instant. Take a trumpet, herald;
Ride thou unto the horsemen on yon hill:
If they will fight with us, bid them come down,
Or void the field; they do offend our sight:
If they'll do neither, we will come to them,
And make them skirr away, as swift as stones
Enforced from the old Assyrian slings:
Besides, we'll cut the throats of those we have,
And not a man of them that we shall take
Shall taste our mercy. Go and tell them so.

Enter MONTJOY

EXETER
Here comes the herald of the French, my liege.

GLOUCESTER
His eyes are humbler than they used to be.

KING HENRY V
How now! what means this, herald? know'st thou not
That I have fined these bones of mine for ransom?
Comest thou again for ransom?

MONTJOY
No, great king:
I come to thee for charitable licence,
That we may wander o'er this bloody field
To look our dead, and then to bury them;
To sort our nobles from our common men.
For many of our princes—woe the while!—
Lie drown'd and soak'd in mercenary blood;
So do our vulgar drench their peasant limbs
In blood of princes; and their wounded steeds
Fret fetlock deep in gore and with wild rage
Yerk out their armed heels at their dead masters,
Killing them twice. O, give us leave, great king,
To view the field in safety and dispose
Of their dead bodies!

KING HENRY V
I tell thee truly, herald,
I know not if the day be ours or no;
For yet a many of your horsemen peer
And gallop o'er the field.

MONTJOY
The day is yours.

KING HENRY V
Praised be God, and not our strength, for it!
What is this castle call'd that stands hard by?

MONTJOY
They call it Agincourt.

KING HENRY V
Then call we this the field of Agincourt,
Fought on the day of Crispin Crispianus.

FLUELLEN
Your grandfather of famous memory, an't please your majesty, and your great-uncle Edward the Plack Prince of Wales, as I have read in the chronicles, fought a most prave pattle here in France.

KING HENRY V
They did, Fluellen.

FLUELLEN
Your majesty says very true: if your majesties is remembered of it, the Welshmen did good service in a garden where leeks did grow, wearing leeks in their Monmouth caps; which, your majesty know, to this hour is an honourable badge of the service; and I do believe your majesty takes no scorn to wear the leek upon Saint Tavy's day.

KING HENRY V
I wear it for a memorable honour;
For I am Welsh, you know, good countryman.

FLUELLEN
All the water in Wye cannot wash your majesty's Welsh plood out of your pody, I can tell you that: God pless it and preserve it, as long as it pleases his grace, and his majesty too!

KING HENRY V
Thanks, good my countryman.

FLUELLEN
By Jeshu, I am your majesty's countryman, I care not who know it; I will confess it to all the 'orld: I need not to be ashamed of your majesty, praised be God, so long as your majesty is an honest man.

KING HENRY V

God keep me so! Our heralds go with him:
Bring me just notice of the numbers dead
On both our parts. Call yonder fellow hither.

Points to WILLIAMS.

Exeunt Heralds with MONTJOY

EXETER
Soldier, you must come to the king.

KING HENRY V
Soldier, why wearest thou that glove in thy cap?

WILLIAMS
An't please your majesty, 'tis the gage of one that
I should fight withal, if he be alive.

KING HENRY V
An Englishman?

WILLIAMS
An't please your majesty, a rascal that swaggered with me last night; who, if alive and ever dare to challenge this glove, I have sworn to take him a box o' th' ear: or if I can see my glove in his cap, which he swore, as he was a soldier, he would wear if alive, I will strike it out soundly.

KING HENRY V
What think you, Captain Fluellen? is it fit this soldier keep his oath?

FLUELLEN
He is a craven and a villain else, an't please your majesty, in my conscience.

KING HENRY V
It may be his enemy is a gentleman of great sort, quite from the answer of his degree.

FLUELLEN
Though he be as good a gentleman as the devil is, as Lucifer and Belzebub himself, it is necessary, look your grace, that he keep his vow and his oath: if he be perjured, see you now, his reputation is as arrant a villain and a Jacksauce, as ever his black shoe trod upon God's ground and his earth, in my conscience, la!

KING HENRY V
Then keep thy vow, sirrah, when thou meetest the fellow.

WILLIAMS
So I will, my liege, as I live.

KING HENRY V
Who servest thou under?

WILLIAMS

Under Captain Gower, my liege.

FLUELLEN
Gower is a good captain, and is good knowledge and literatured in the wars.

KING HENRY V
Call him hither to me, soldier.

WILLIAMS
I will, my liege.

Exit

KING HENRY V
Here, Fluellen; wear thou this favour for me and stick it in thy cap: when Alencon and myself were down together, I plucked this glove from his helm: if any man challenge this, he is a friend to Alencon, and an enemy to our person; if thou encounter any such, apprehend him, an thou dost me love.

FLUELLEN
Your grace doo's me as great honours as can be desired in the hearts of his subjects: I would fain see the man, that has but two legs, that shall find himself aggrieved at this glove; that is all; but I would fain see it once, an please God of his grace that I might see.

KING HENRY V
Knowest thou Gower?

FLUELLEN
He is my dear friend, an please you.

KING HENRY V
Pray thee, go seek him, and bring him to my tent.

FLUELLEN
I will fetch him.

Exit

KING HENRY V
My Lord of Warwick, and my brother Gloucester,
Follow Fluellen closely at the heels:
The glove which I have given him for a favour
May haply purchase him a box o' th' ear;
It is the soldier's; I by bargain should
Wear it myself. Follow, good cousin Warwick:
If that the soldier strike him, as I judge
By his blunt bearing he will keep his word,
Some sudden mischief may arise of it;
For I do know Fluellen valiant
And, touched with choler, hot as gunpowder,
And quickly will return an injury:

Follow and see there be no harm between them.
Go you with me, uncle of Exeter.

Exeunt

SCENE VIII. Before King Henry'S Pavilion.

Enter GOWER and WILLIAMS

WILLIAMS
I warrant it is to knight you, captain.

Enter FLUELLEN

FLUELLEN
God's will and his pleasure, captain, I beseech you now, come apace to the king: there is more good toward you peradventure than is in your knowledge to dream of.

WILLIAMS
Sir, know you this glove?

FLUELLEN
Know the glove! I know the glove is glove.

WILLIAMS
I know this; and thus I challenge it.

Strikes him

FLUELLEN
'Sblood! an arrant traitor as any is in the universal world, or in France, or in England!

GOWER
How now, sir! you villain!

WILLIAMS
Do you think I'll be forsworn?

FLUELLEN
Stand away, Captain Gower; I will give treason his payment into ploughs, I warrant you.

WILLIAMS
I am no traitor.

FLUELLEN
That's a lie in thy throat. I charge you in his majesty's name, apprehend him: he's a friend of the Duke Alencon's.

Enter WARWICK and GLOUCESTER

WARWICK
How now, how now! what's the matter?

FLUELLEN
My Lord of Warwick, here is—praised be God for it!—a most contagious treason come to light, look you, as you shall desire in a summer's day. Here is his majesty.

Enter KING HENRY and EXETER

KING HENRY V
How now! what's the matter?

FLUELLEN
My liege, here is a villain and a traitor, that, look your grace, has struck the glove which your majesty is take out of the helmet of Alencon.

WILLIAMS
My liege, this was my glove; here is the fellow of it; and he that I gave it to in change promised to wear it in his cap: I promised to strike him, if he did: I met this man with my glove in his cap, and I have been as good as my word.

FLUELLEN
Your majesty hear now, saving your majesty's manhood, what an arrant, rascally, beggarly, lousy knave it is: I hope your majesty is pear me testimony and witness, and will avouchment, that this is the glove of Alencon, that your majesty is give me; in your conscience, now?

KING HENRY V
Give me thy glove, soldier: look, here is the fellow of it.
'Twas I, indeed, thou promised'st to strike;
And thou hast given me most bitter terms.

FLUELLEN
An please your majesty, let his neck answer for it, if there is any martial law in the world.

KING HENRY V
How canst thou make me satisfaction?

WILLIAMS
All offences, my lord, come from the heart: never came any from mine that might offend your majesty.

KING HENRY V
It was ourself thou didst abuse.

WILLIAMS
Your majesty came not like yourself: you appeared to me but as a common man; witness the night, your garments, your lowliness; and what your highness suffered under that shape, I beseech you take it for your own fault and not mine: for had you been as I took you for, I made no offence; therefore, I beseech your highness, pardon me.

KING HENRY V
Here, uncle Exeter, fill this glove with crowns,
And give it to this fellow. Keep it, fellow;
And wear it for an honour in thy cap
Till I do challenge it. Give him the crowns:
And, captain, you must needs be friends with him.

FLUELLEN
By this day and this light, the fellow has mettle enough in his belly. Hold, there is twelve pence for you; and I pray you to serve Got, and keep you out of prawls, and prabbles' and quarrels, and dissensions, and, I warrant you, it is the better for you.

WILLIAMS
I will none of your money.

FLUELLEN
It is with a good will; I can tell you, it will serve you to mend your shoes: come, wherefore should you be so pashful? your shoes is not so good: 'tis a good silling, I warrant you, or I will change it.

Enter an English HERALD

KING HENRY V
Now, herald, are the dead number'd?

HERALD
Here is the number of the slaughter'd French.

KING HENRY V
What prisoners of good sort are taken, uncle?

EXETER
Charles Duke of Orleans, nephew to the king;
John Duke of Bourbon, and Lord Bouciqualt:
Of other lords and barons, knights and squires,
Full fifteen hundred, besides common men.

KING HENRY V
This note doth tell me of ten thousand French
That in the field lie slain: of princes, in this number,
And nobles bearing banners, there lie dead
One hundred twenty six: added to these,
Of knights, esquires, and gallant gentlemen,
Eight thousand and four hundred; of the which,
Five hundred were but yesterday dubb'd knights:
So that, in these ten thousand they have lost,
There are but sixteen hundred mercenaries;
The rest are princes, barons, lords, knights, squires,
And gentlemen of blood and quality.
The names of those their nobles that lie dead:
Charles Delabreth, high constable of France;
Jaques of Chatillon, admiral of France;

The master of the cross-bows, Lord Rambures;
Great Master of France, the brave Sir Guichard Dolphin,
John Duke of Alencon, Anthony Duke of Brabant,
The brother of the Duke of Burgundy,
And Edward Duke of Bar: of lusty earls,
Grandpre and Roussi, Fauconberg and Foix,
Beaumont and Marle, Vaudemont and Lestrale.
Here was a royal fellowship of death!
Where is the number of our English dead?
Herald shews him another paper
Edward the Duke of York, the Earl of Suffolk,
Sir Richard Ketly, Davy Gam, esquire:
None else of name; and of all other men
But five and twenty. O God, thy arm was here;
And not to us, but to thy arm alone,
Ascribe we all! When, without stratagem,
But in plain shock and even play of battle,
Was ever known so great and little loss
On one part and on the other? Take it, God,
For it is none but thine!

EXETER
'Tis wonderful!

KING HENRY V
Come, go we in procession to the village.
And be it death proclaimed through our host
To boast of this or take the praise from God
Which is his only.

FLUELLEN
Is it not lawful, an please your majesty, to tell how many is killed?

KING HENRY V
Yes, captain; but with this acknowledgement,
That God fought for us.

FLUELLEN
Yes, my conscience, he did us great good.

KING HENRY V
Do we all holy rites;
Let there be sung 'Non nobis' and 'Te Deum;'
The dead with charity enclosed in clay:
And then to Calais; and to England then:
Where ne'er from France arrived more happy men.

Exeunt

ACT V

PROLOGUE

Enter CHORUS

CHORUS
Vouchsafe to those that have not read the story,
That I may prompt them: and of such as have,
I humbly pray them to admit the excuse
Of time, of numbers and due course of things,
Which cannot in their huge and proper life
Be here presented. Now we bear the king
Toward Calais: grant him there; there seen,
Heave him away upon your winged thoughts
Athwart the sea. Behold, the English beach
Pales in the flood with men, with wives and boys,
Whose shouts and claps out-voice the deep mouth'd sea,
Which like a mighty whiffler 'fore the king
Seems to prepare his way: so let him land,
And solemnly see him set on to London.
So swift a pace hath thought that even now
You may imagine him upon Blackheath;
Where that his lords desire him to have borne
His bruised helmet and his bended sword
Before him through the city: he forbids it,
Being free from vainness and self-glorious pride;
Giving full trophy, signal and ostent
Quite from himself to God. But now behold,
In the quick forge and working-house of thought,
How London doth pour out her citizens!
The mayor and all his brethren in best sort,
Like to the senators of the antique Rome,
With the plebeians swarming at their heels,
Go forth and fetch their conquering Caesar in:
As, by a lower but loving likelihood,
Were now the general of our gracious empress,
As in good time he may, from Ireland coming,
Bringing rebellion broached on his sword,
How many would the peaceful city quit,
To welcome him! much more, and much more cause,
Did they this Harry. Now in London place him;
As yet the lamentation of the French
Invites the King of England's stay at home;
The emperor's coming in behalf of France,
To order peace between them; and omit
All the occurrences, whatever chanced,
Till Harry's back-return again to France:
There must we bring him; and myself have play'd
The interim, by remembering you 'tis past.

Then brook abridgment, and your eyes advance,
After your thoughts, straight back again to France.

Exit

SCENE I. France. The English Camp

Enter FLUELLEN and GOWER

GOWER
Nay, that's right; but why wear you your leek today?
Saint Davy's day is past.

FLUELLEN
There is occasions and causes why and wherefore in all things: I will tell you, asse my friend, Captain Gower: the rascally, scald, beggarly, lousy, pragging knave, Pistol, which you and yourself and all the world know to be no petter than a fellow, look you now, of no merits, he is come to me and prings me pread and salt yesterday, look you, and bid me eat my leek: it was in place where I could not breed no contention with him; but I will be so bold as to wear it in my cap till I see him once again, and then I will tell him a little piece of my desires.

Enter PISTOL

GOWER
Why, here he comes, swelling like a turkey-cock.

FLUELLEN
'Tis no matter for his swellings nor his turkey-cocks. God pless you, Aunchient Pistol! You scurvy, lousy knave, God pless you!

PISTOL
Ha! art thou bedlam? dost thou thirst, base Trojan,
To have me fold up Parca's fatal web?
Hence! I am qualmish at the smell of leek.

FLUELLEN
I peseech you heartily, scurvy, lousy knave, at my desires, and my requests, and my petitions, to eat, look you, this leek: because, look you, you do not love it, nor your affections and your appetites and your digestions doo's not agree with it, I would desire you to eat it.

PISTOL
Not for Cadwallader and all his goats.

FLUELLEN
There is one goat for you.

Strikes him

Will you be so good, scauld knave, as eat it?

PISTOL
Base Trojan, thou shalt die.

FLUELLEN
You say very true, scauld knave, when God's will is: I will desire you to live in the mean time, and eat your victuals: come, there is sauce for it.

Strikes him

You called me yesterday mountain-squire; but I will make you to-day a squire of low degree. I pray you, fall to: if you can mock a leek, you can eat a leek.

GOWER
Enough, captain: you have astonished him.

FLUELLEN
I say, I will make him eat some part of my leek, or I will peat his pate four days. Bite, I pray you; it is good for your green wound and your ploody coxcomb.

PISTOL
Must I bite?

FLUELLEN
Yes, certainly, and out of doubt and out of question too, and ambiguities.

PISTOL
By this leek, I will most horribly revenge: I eat and eat, I swear—

FLUELLEN
Eat, I pray you: will you have some more sauce to your leek? there is not enough leek to swear by.

PISTOL
Quiet thy cudgel; thou dost see I eat.

FLUELLEN
Much good do you, scauld knave, heartily. Nay, pray you, throw none away; the skin is good for your broken coxcomb. When you take occasions to see leeks hereafter, I pray you, mock at 'em; that is all.

PISTOL
Good.

FLUELLEN
Ay, leeks is good: hold you, there is a groat to heal your pate.

PISTOL
Me a groat!

FLUELLEN
Yes, verily and in truth, you shall take it; or I have another leek in my pocket, which you shall eat.

PISTOL
I take thy groat in earnest of revenge.

FLUELLEN
If I owe you any thing, I will pay you in cudgels: you shall be a woodmonger, and buy nothing of me but cudgels. God b' wi' you, and keep you, and heal your pate.

Exit

PISTOL
All hell shall stir for this.

GOWER
Go, go; you are a counterfeit cowardly knave. Will you mock at an ancient tradition, begun upon an honourable respect, and worn as a memorable trophy of predeceased valour and dare not avouch in your deeds any of your words? I have seen you gleeking and galling at this gentleman twice or thrice. You thought, because he could not speak English in the native garb, he could not therefore handle an English cudgel: you find it otherwise; and henceforth let a Welsh correction teach you a good English condition. Fare ye well.

Exit

PISTOL
Doth Fortune play the huswife with me now?
News have I, that my Nell is dead i' the spital
Of malady of France;
And there my rendezvous is quite cut off.
Old I do wax; and from my weary limbs
Honour is cudgelled. Well, bawd I'll turn,
And something lean to cutpurse of quick hand.
To England will I steal, and there I'll steal:
And patches will I get unto these cudgell'd scars,
And swear I got them in the Gallia wars.

Exit

SCENE II. France. A Royal Palace

Enter, at one door KING HENRY, EXETER, BEDFORD, GLOUCESTER, WARWICK, WESTMORELAND, and other Lords; at another, the FRENCH KING, QUEEN ISABEL, the PRINCESS KATHARINE, ALICE and other Ladies; the DUKE of BURGUNDY, and his train

KING HENRY V
Peace to this meeting, wherefore we are met!
Unto our brother France, and to our sister,
Health and fair time of day; joy and good wishes
To our most fair and princely cousin Katharine;
And, as a branch and member of this royalty,
By whom this great assembly is contrived,

We do salute you, Duke of Burgundy;
And, princes French, and peers, health to you all!

KING OF FRANCE
Right joyous are we to behold your face,
Most worthy brother England; fairly met:
So are you, princes English, every one.

QUEEN ISABEL
So happy be the issue, brother England,
Of this good day and of this gracious meeting,
As we are now glad to behold your eyes;
Your eyes, which hitherto have borne in them
Against the French, that met them in their bent,
The fatal balls of murdering basilisks:
The venom of such looks, we fairly hope,
Have lost their quality, and that this day
Shall change all griefs and quarrels into love.

KING HENRY V
To cry amen to that, thus we appear.

QUEEN ISABEL
You English princes all, I do salute you.

BURGUNDY
My duty to you both, on equal love,
Great Kings of France and England! That I have labour'd,
With all my wits, my pains and strong endeavours,
To bring your most imperial majesties
Unto this bar and royal interview,
Your mightiness on both parts best can witness.
Since then my office hath so far prevail'd
That, face to face and royal eye to eye,
You have congreeted, let it not disgrace me,
If I demand, before this royal view,
What rub or what impediment there is,
Why that the naked, poor and mangled Peace,
Dear nurse of arts and joyful births,
Should not in this best garden of the world
Our fertile France, put up her lovely visage?
Alas, she hath from France too long been chased,
And all her husbandry doth lie on heaps,
Corrupting in its own fertility.
Her vine, the merry cheerer of the heart,
Unpruned dies; her hedges even-pleach'd,
Like prisoners wildly overgrown with hair,
Put forth disorder'd twigs; her fallow leas
The darnel, hemlock and rank fumitory
Doth root upon, while that the coulter rusts
That should deracinate such savagery;

The even mead, that erst brought sweetly forth
The freckled cowslip, burnet and green clover,
Wanting the scythe, all uncorrected, rank,
Conceives by idleness and nothing teems
But hateful docks, rough thistles, kecksies, burs,
Losing both beauty and utility.
And as our vineyards, fallows, meads and hedges,
Defective in their natures, grow to wildness,
Even so our houses and ourselves and children
Have lost, or do not learn for want of time,
The sciences that should become our country;
But grow like savages, as soldiers will
That nothing do but meditate on blood,
To swearing and stern looks, diffused attire
And every thing that seems unnatural.
Which to reduce into our former favour
You are assembled: and my speech entreats
That I may know the let, why gentle Peace
Should not expel these inconveniences
And bless us with her former qualities.

KING HENRY V
If, Duke of Burgundy, you would the peace,
Whose want gives growth to the imperfections
Which you have cited, you must buy that peace
With full accord to all our just demands;
Whose tenors and particular effects
You have enscheduled briefly in your hands.

BURGUNDY
The king hath heard them; to the which as yet
There is no answer made.

KING HENRY V
Well then the peace,
Which you before so urged, lies in his answer.

KING OF FRANCE
I have but with a cursorary eye
O'erglanced the articles: pleaseth your grace
To appoint some of your council presently
To sit with us once more, with better heed
To re-survey them, we will suddenly
Pass our accept and peremptory answer.

KING HENRY V
Brother, we shall. Go, uncle Exeter,
And brother Clarence, and you, brother Gloucester,
Warwick and Huntingdon, go with the king;
And take with you free power to ratify,
Augment, or alter, as your wisdoms best

Shall see advantageable for our dignity,
Any thing in or out of our demands,
And we'll consign thereto. Will you, fair sister,
Go with the princes, or stay here with us?

QUEEN ISABEL
Our gracious brother, I will go with them:
Haply a woman's voice may do some good,
When articles too nicely urged be stood on.

KING HENRY V
Yet leave our cousin Katharine here with us:
She is our capital demand, comprised
Within the fore-rank of our articles.

QUEEN ISABEL
She hath good leave.

Exeunt all except HENRY, KATHARINE, and ALICE

KING HENRY V
Fair Katharine, and most fair,
Will you vouchsafe to teach a soldier terms
Such as will enter at a lady's ear
And plead his love-suit to her gentle heart?

KATHARINE
Your majesty shall mock at me; I cannot speak your England.

KING HENRY V
O fair Katharine, if you will love me soundly with your French heart, I will be glad to hear you confess it brokenly with your English tongue. Do you like me, Kate?

KATHARINE
Pardonnez-moi, I cannot tell vat is 'like me.'

KING HENRY V
An angel is like you, Kate, and you are like an angel.

KATHARINE
Que dit-il? que je suis semblable a les anges?

ALICE
Oui, vraiment, sauf votre grace, ainsi dit-il.

KING HENRY V
I said so, dear Katharine; and I must not blush to affirm it.

KATHARINE
O bon Dieu! les langues des hommes sont pleines de tromperies.

KING HENRY V
What says she, fair one? that the tongues of men are full of deceits?

ALICE
Oui, dat de tongues of de mans is be full of deceits: dat is de princess.

KING HENRY V
The princess is the better Englishwoman. I' faith, Kate, my wooing is fit for thy understanding: I am glad thou canst speak no better English; for, if thou couldst, thou wouldst find me such a plain king that thou wouldst think I had sold my farm to buy my crown. I know no ways to mince it in love, but directly to say 'I love you:' then if you urge me farther than to say 'do you in faith?' I wear out my suit. Give me your answer; i' faith, do: and so clap hands and a bargain: how say you, lady?

KATHARINE
Sauf votre honneur, me understand vell.

KING HENRY V
Marry, if you would put me to verses or to dance for your sake, Kate, why you undid me: for the one, I have neither words nor measure, and for the other, I have no strength in measure, yet a reasonable measure in strength. If I could win a lady at leap-frog, or by vaulting into my saddle with my armour on my back, under the correction of bragging be it spoken. I should quickly leap into a wife. Or if I might buffet for my love, or bound my horse for her favours, I could lay on like a butcher and sit like a jack-an-apes, never off. But, before God, Kate, I cannot look greenly nor gasp out my eloquence, nor I have no cunning in protestation; only downright oaths, which I never use till urged, nor never break for urging. If thou canst love a fellow of this temper, Kate, whose face is not worth sun-burning, that never looks in his glass for love of any thing he sees there, let thine eye be thy cook. I speak to thee plain soldier: If thou canst love me for this, take me: if not, to say to thee that I shall die, is true; but for thy love, by the Lord, no; yet I love thee too. And while thou livest, dear Kate, take a fellow of plain and uncoined constancy; for he perforce must do thee right, because he hath not the gift to woo in other places: for these fellows of infinite tongue, that can rhyme themselves into ladies' favours, they do always reason themselves out again. What! a speaker is but a prater; a rhyme is but a ballad. A good leg will fall; a straight back will stoop; a black beard will turn white; a curled pate will grow bald; a fair face will wither; a full eye will wax hollow: but a good heart, Kate, is the sun and the moon; or, rather, the sun, and not the moon; for it shines bright and never changes, but keeps his course truly. If thou would have such a one, take me; and take me, take a soldier; take a soldier, take a king. And what sayest thou then to my love? speak, my fair, and fairly, I pray thee.

KATHARINE
Is it possible dat I sould love de enemy of France?

KING HENRY V
No; it is not possible you should love the enemy of France, Kate: but, in loving me, you should love the friend of France; for I love France so well that I will not part with a village of it; I will have it all mine: and, Kate, when France is mine and I am yours, then yours is France and you are mine.

KATHARINE
I cannot tell vat is dat.

KING HENRY V

No, Kate? I will tell thee in French; which I am sure will hang upon my tongue like a new-married wife about her husband's neck, hardly to be shook off. Je quand sur le possession de France, et quand vous avez le possession de moi, let me see, what then? Saint Denis be my speed!—donc votre est France et vous etes mienne. It is as easy for me, Kate, to conquer the kingdom as to speak so much more French: I shall never move thee in French, unless it be to laugh at me.

KATHARINE
Sauf votre honneur, le Francois que vous parlez, il est meilleur que l'Anglois lequel je parle.

KING HENRY V
No, faith, is't not, Kate: but thy speaking of my tongue, and I thine, most truly-falsely, must needs be granted to be much at one. But, Kate, dost thou understand thus much English, canst thou love me?

KATHARINE
I cannot tell.

KING HENRY V
Can any of your neighbours tell, Kate? I'll ask them. Come, I know thou lovest me: and at night, when you come into your closet, you'll question this gentlewoman about me; and I know, Kate, you will to her dispraise those parts in me that you love with your heart: but, good Kate, mock me mercifully; the rather, gentle princess, because I love thee cruelly. If ever thou beest mine, Kate, as I have a saving faith within me tells me thou shalt, I get thee with scambling, and thou must therefore needs prove a good soldier-breeder: shall not thou and I, between Saint Denis and Saint George, compound a boy, half French, half English, that shall go to Constantinople and take the Turk by the beard? shall we not? what sayest thou, my fair flower-de-luce?

KATHARINE
I do not know dat

KING HENRY V
No; 'tis hereafter to know, but now to promise: do but now promise, Kate, you will endeavour for your French part of such a boy; and for my English moiety take the word of a king and a bachelor. How answer you, la plus belle Katharine du monde, mon tres cher et devin deesse?

KATHARINE
Your majestee ave fausse French enough to deceive de most sage demoiselle dat is en France.

KING HENRY V
Now, fie upon my false French! By mine honour, in true English, I love thee, Kate: by which honour I dare not swear thou lovest me; yet my blood begins to flatter me that thou dost, notwithstanding the poor and untempering effect of my visage. Now, beshrew my father's ambition! he was thinking of civil wars when he got me: therefore was I created with a stubborn outside, with an aspect of iron, that, when I come to woo ladies, I fright them. But, in faith, Kate, the elder I wax, the better I shall appear: my comfort is, that old age, that ill layer up of beauty, can do no more, spoil upon my face: thou hast me, if thou hast me, at the worst; and thou shalt wear me, if thou wear me, better and better: and therefore tell me, most fair Katharine, will you have me? Put off your maiden blushes; avouch the thoughts of your heart with the looks of an empress; take me by the hand, and say 'Harry of England I am thine:' which word thou shalt no sooner bless mine ear withal, but I will tell thee aloud 'England is thine, Ireland is thine, France is thine, and Harry Plantagenet is thine;' who though I speak it before his face, if he be not fellow with the best king, thou shalt find the best king

of good fellows. Come, your answer in broken music; for thy voice is music and thy English broken; therefore, queen of all, Katharine, break thy mind to me in broken English; wilt thou have me?

KATHARINE
Dat is as it sall please de roi mon pere.

KING HENRY V
Nay, it will please him well, Kate it shall please him, Kate.

KATHARINE
Den it sall also content me.

KING HENRY V
Upon that I kiss your hand, and I call you my queen.

KATHARINE
Laissez, mon seigneur, laissez, laissez: ma foi, je ne veux point que vous abaissiez votre grandeur en baisant la main d'une de votre seigeurie indigne serviteur; excusez-moi, je vous supplie, mon tres-puissant seigneur.

KING HENRY V
Then I will kiss your lips, Kate.

KATHARINE
Les dames et demoiselles pour etre baisees devant leur noces, il n'est pas la coutume de France.

KING HENRY V
Madam my interpreter, what says she?

ALICE
Dat it is not be de fashion pour les ladies of France, I cannot tell vat is baiser en Anglish.

KING HENRY V
To kiss.

ALICE
Your majesty entendre bettre que moi.

KING HENRY V
It is not a fashion for the maids in France to kiss before they are married, would she say?

ALICE
Oui, vraiment.

KING HENRY V
O Kate, nice customs curtsy to great kings. Dear Kate, you and I cannot be confined within the weak list of a country's fashion: we are the makers of manners, Kate; and the liberty that follows our places stops the mouth of all find-faults; as I will do yours, for upholding the nice fashion of your country in denying me a kiss: therefore, patiently and yielding.

Kissing her

You have witchcraft in your lips, Kate: there is more eloquence in a sugar touch of them than in the tongues of the French council; and they should sooner persuade Harry of England than a general petition of monarchs. Here comes your father.

Re-enter the FRENCH KING and his QUEEN, BURGUNDY, and other Lords

BURGUNDY
God save your majesty! my royal cousin, teach you our princess English?

KING HENRY V
I would have her learn, my fair cousin, how perfectly I love her; and that is good English.

BURGUNDY
Is she not apt?

KING HENRY V
Our tongue is rough, coz, and my condition is not smooth; so that, having neither the voice nor the heart of flattery about me, I cannot so conjure up the spirit of love in her, that he will appear in his true likeness.

BURGUNDY
Pardon the frankness of my mirth, if I answer you for that. If you would conjure in her, you must make a circle; if conjure up love in her in his true likeness, he must appear naked and blind. Can you blame her then, being a maid yet rosed over with the virgin crimson of modesty, if she deny the appearance of a naked blind boy in her naked seeing self? It were, my lord, a hard condition for a maid to consign to.

KING HENRY V
Yet they do wink and yield, as love is blind and enforces.

BURGUNDY
They are then excused, my lord, when they see not what they do.

KING HENRY V
Then, good my lord, teach your cousin to consent winking.

BURGUNDY
I will wink on her to consent, my lord, if you will teach her to know my meaning: for maids, well summered and warm kept, are like flies at Bartholomew-tide, blind, though they have their eyes; and then they will endure handling, which before would not abide looking on.

KING HENRY V
This moral ties me over to time and a hot summer; and so I shall catch the fly, your cousin, in the latter end and she must be blind too.

BURGUNDY
As love is, my lord, before it loves.

KING HENRY V

It is so: and you may, some of you, thank love for my blindness, who cannot see many a fair French city for one fair French maid that stands in my way.

FRENCH KING
Yes, my lord, you see them perspectively, the cities turned into a maid; for they are all girdled with maiden walls that war hath never entered.

KING HENRY V
Shall Kate be my wife?

FRENCH KING
So please you.

KING HENRY V
I am content; so the maiden cities you talk of may wait on her: so the maid that stood in the way for my wish shall show me the way to my will.

FRENCH KING
We have consented to all terms of reason.

KING HENRY V
Is't so, my lords of England?

WESTMORELAND
The king hath granted every article:
His daughter first, and then in sequel all,
According to their firm proposed natures.

EXETER
Only he hath not yet subscribed this: Where your majesty demands, that the King of France, having any occasion to write for matter of grant, shall name your highness in this form and with this addition in French, Notre trescher fils Henri, Roi d'Angleterre, Heritier de France; and thus in Latin, Praeclarissimus filius noster Henricus, Rex Angliae, et Haeres Franciae.

FRENCH KING
Nor this I have not, brother, so denied,
But your request shall make me let it pass.

KING HENRY V
I pray you then, in love and dear alliance,
Let that one article rank with the rest;
And thereupon give me your daughter.

FRENCH KING
Take her, fair son, and from her blood raise up
Issue to me; that the contending kingdoms
Of France and England, whose very shores look pale
With envy of each other's happiness,
May cease their hatred, and this dear conjunction
Plant neighbourhood and Christian-like accord

In their sweet bosoms, that never war advance
His bleeding sword 'twixt England and fair France.

ALL
Amen!

KING HENRY V
Now, welcome, Kate: and bear me witness all,
That here I kiss her as my sovereign queen.

Flourish

QUEEN ISABEL
God, the best maker of all marriages,
Combine your hearts in one, your realms in one!
As man and wife, being two, are one in love,
So be there 'twixt your kingdoms such a spousal,
That never may ill office, or fell jealousy,
Which troubles oft the bed of blessed marriage,
Thrust in between the paction of these kingdoms,
To make divorce of their incorporate league;
That English may as French, French Englishmen,
Receive each other. God speak this Amen!

ALL
Amen!

KING HENRY V
Prepare we for our marriage—on which day,
My Lord of Burgundy, we'll take your oath,
And all the peers', for surety of our leagues.
Then shall I swear to Kate, and you to me;
And may our oaths well kept and prosperous be!

Sennet.

Exeunt

EPILOGUE

Enter CHORUS

CHORUS
Thus far, with rough and all-unable pen,
Our bending author hath pursued the story,
In little room confining mighty men,
Mangling by starts the full course of their glory.
Small time, but in that small most greatly lived
This star of England: Fortune made his sword;

By which the world's best garden be achieved,
And of it left his son imperial lord.
Henry the Sixth, in infant bands crown'd King
Of France and England, did this king succeed;
Whose state so many had the managing,
That they lost France and made his England bleed:
Which oft our stage hath shown; and, for their sake,
In your fair minds let this acceptance take.

Exit

William Shakespeare – A Short Biography

The life of William Shakespeare, arguably the most significant figure in the Western literary canon, is relatively unknown. Even the exact date of his birth is uncertain. April 23rd, the date now generally accepted to be the date of his birth, is a result of a scholarly mistake and the appealing coincidence of its being also the day of his death.

That so little is known about a writer with such great literary scope and accomplishment has naturally invited speculation and conspiracy theories about the authenticity of his authorship, his influence and even his existence.

Shakespeare was born in Stratford-upon-Avon in 1565, possibly on the 23rd April, St. George's Day, and baptised there on 26th April. His father was John Shakespeare, a successful glover and alderman who hailed from Snitterfield. His mother was Mary Arden, whose father was an affluent landowner. In total their union bore eight children; William was the third of these and the eldest surviving son.

Although there is no hard evidence on his education it is widely agreed among scholars that William attended the King's New School in Stratford which was chartered as a free school in 1553. This school was only a quarter of a mile from the house in which he spent his childhood, but since there are no attendance records existing it is assumed, rather than known, this was the base for his education.

Although the quality of education in a grammar school at that time varied wildly the curriculum did not, a key aspect of which, by royal decree, was Latin, and it is undoubtable that the school will have delivered an intensive education in Latin grammar, drawing heavily on the work of the classical Latin authors. If Shakespeare did attend this school then it is very likely the starting point for the fascination with and extensive knowledge of the classical Latin authors which would inform and inspire so much of his work began.

Little more detail is known of William's childhood, or his early teenage years, until, at the age of 18, he married Anne Hathaway, who was 26 and from the nearby village of Shottery. Her father was a yeoman farmer, and their family home a small farmhouse in the village. In his will he left her £6 13s 4d, six pounds, thirteen shillings and fourpence, to be paid on her wedding day. On November 27th, 1582 the consistory court of the Diocese of Worcester issued a marriage licence, and on the 28th two of Hathaway's neighbours, Fulk Sandells and John Richardson, posted bonds which guaranteed that there were no lawful claims to impede the marriage along with a surety of £40 to act as a financial guarantee for the wedding.

The marriage was conducted in some haste since, unusually, the marriage banns were read only once instead of the more normal three times, a decision which would have been taken by the Worcester chancellor. This haste is no doubt due to the child Anne delivered their first child, Susanna, six months later. Susanna, was baptised on May 26th, 1583. Several scholars have voiced their opinion that the wedding was imposed on a reluctant Shakespeare by Hathaway's outraged parents, although, again, there is nothing to formally support the theory. It has been further argued that the circumstances surrounding the wedding, particularly those of the neighbourly assurances, indicate that Shakespeare was involved with two women at the time of his marriage. According to the theory proposed by the early twentieth century scholar Frank Harris, Shakespeare had already chosen to marry a woman named Anne Whateley. It was only once this proposed union became known that Hathaway's outraged family forced him to marry their daughter. Harris goes on to surmise that Shakespeare considered the affair entrapment, and that this led to his wholesale despising of her, a "loathing for his wife [which] was measureless" and which ultimately caused him to leave Stratford and her and make for the theatre. But equally other scholars such as John Aubrey have responded to this with evidence that Shakespeare returned to Stratford every year which, if true, would rather diminish Harris's claim that Hathaway had poisoned Stratford for Shakespeare.

Harris's theory aside, Shakespeare and Hathaway had two more children, twins Hamnet and Judith, baptised on February 2nd,1585. Hamnet, Shakespeare's only son, died during one of the frequent outbreaks of bubonic plague and was buried on the August 11th, 1596, at the age of only eleven.

Little is known of Shakespeare's life during the years following the birth of the twins until he appears mentioned in relation to the London theatres in 1592, apart from a fleeting mention in the complaints bill of a legal case which came before the Queen's Bench court at Westminster, dated Michaelmas Term 1588 and October 9th, 1589. Despite this period of time being referred to in scholarly circles as Shakespeare's "lost years", there are several stories, apocryphal in nature, which are attributed to Shakespeare. For example, there is a legend in Stratford that he fled the town in order to avoid prosecution for poaching deer on the estate of Thomas Lucy, a local squire. It is also supposed that Shakespeare went so far as to take revenge on Lucy, a politician whose Protestantism opposed Shakespeare's Catholic childhood, by writing the following lampooning ballad about him:

> A parliament member, a justice of peace,
> At home a poor scarecrow, at London an ass,
> If lousy is Lucy as some folks miscall it
> Then Lucy is lousy whatever befall it.

However amusing the ballad and legend may be in imagining the life of a young Shakespeare, youthfully mischievous and still developing the wit, sense of adventure and humour which would become integral aspects of his writing, there is simply no evidence either to support the theory or to suggest that Shakespeare penned the ballad. Alongside this are suggestions that he began his theatrical career while minding the horses of the patrons of the London theatres and that he spent some time as a schoolmaster employed by one Alexander Hoghton, a Catholic landowner in Lancashire, in whose will is named "William Shakeshafte". However, this was a popular name in the Lancashire area at that time and there is no evidence that this referred to Shakespeare. The wealth of his writing makes it a frustrating exercise to learn more of his life and the manner in which he achieved those outstanding and lionized works.

Interestingly, the reference to Shakespeare in 1592 which ends the "lost years" is a piece of theatrical criticism by playwright Robert Greene in *Groats-Worth of Wit*. In a scathing passage Greene writes "…there is an upstart Crow, beautified with our feathers, that with his *Tiger's heart wrapped in a Player's hide*, supposes he is as well able to bombast out a blank verse as the best of you: and being an absolute *Johannes factotum*, is in his own conceit the only Shake-scene in a country." From this entry we can make some important inferences which shed light on Shakespeare's career, the first of which is that to be acknowledged, even negatively, by a playwright such as Robert Greene, by this point he must have been making significant impact on the London stage as a writer. Also of significance is the very meaning of the words themselves, for it is generally acknowledged that Shakespeare is being accused of writing with a lofty ambition beyond his capabilities and, more importantly, the capabilities of his contemporaries who were educated at Oxford and Cambridge. Within this remark, then, is an inherent snobbery which Shakespeare would come to resent and ultimately challenge in his writing. Though Greene's parody of "Oh, tiger's heart wrapped in a woman's hide" makes reference to *Henry VI, Part 3*, it is likely that Greene's opinion of Shakespeare was in part informed by another of Shakespeare's plays which was heavily criticised, *Titus Adronicus*, believed to have been written between 1588 and 1593. It was his first attempt at tragedy, almost prototypical, and was written at a time when, according to the scholar Jonathan Bate, he was "experimenting with ways of writing about and representing rape and seduction". Drawing heavily on the sixth book of Ovid's *Metamorphoses* as its main source of inspiration for the rape and mutilation of Lavinia, it offended the sensibilities of the more highbrow members of its audience, whilst presumably also simultaneously intimidating them with its detailed knowledge of Ovid, a writer typically considered the reserve of the university-educated. Not only, then, was Shakespeare demonstrating a knowledge of classical literature which they thought befitted only a traditional scholar and thereby shining a light to the snobbery and exclusivity of such an education, but he was doing it radically and brilliantly.

By 1594 the Lord Chamberlain's Men had recognised his worthiness as a playwright and were performing his works. With the advantage of Shakespeare's progressive writing they rapidly became London's leading company of players, affording him more exposure and, following the death of Queen Elizabeth in 1603, a royal patent by the new king, James I, at which point they changed their name to the King's Men.

Before this success, though, several company members had formed a partnership to build their own theatre which came to be on the south bank of the river Thames, the now-famous and reconstructed Globe theatre. Though it is unclear precisely what Shakespeare's involvement in this venture was, records of his property and investments indicate that he came to be rich during this period, buying the second-largest house in Stratford, called New Place, in 1597, which he made his family home. Prior to this he was living in the parish of St Helen's Bishopsgate, north of the River Thames. He continued to spend most of his time at work in London and from about 1598-1602, he seems to have lived in the Paris Gardens area of Bankside south of the river near The Globe.

Despite efforts to pirate his work, Shakespeare's name was by 1598 so well known that it had already become a selling point in its own right on title pages.

An interesting aside is that theatres were mostly constructed on the south bank of the Thames (then part of the county of Surrey) as performing in London itself was thought to be a bad influence on the masses and subject to periodic bouts of censorship, repression and closing of venues which in the City itself was mainly courtyards and open areas at the many Inns.

Excluded from the City purpose built theatres began to be constructed outside the City limits. This area of the Thames though was rough and naturally vibrant with all sorts of characters, many of them of dubious nature or even criminal. It was also prone, due to its over-crowding and bad sanitation, to bouts of bubonic plague and other diseases particularly during the summer which was a further reason for the theatres there being closed. The Curtain, The Rose, The Swan, The Fortune,

The Blackfriars and of course The Globe were all purpose built and situated here, some with an audience capacity approaching 3,000.

The first known printed copies of Shakespeare's plays date from 1594 in quarto editions, though these quarto editions are often considered "bad", a term referring to the likelihood of specific quarto editions being based on, for example, a reconstruction of a play as it was witnessed, rather than Shakespeare's original manuscript. The best example of such memorial reconstruction can be found in the differences between the first and second quarto editions of *Hamlet*. In examining Hamlet's most famous soliloquy, "to be or not to be", we can immediately recognise significant differences. First, the familiar second quarto version:

> To be, or not to be; that is the question:
> Whether 'tis nobler in the mind to suffer
> The slings and arrows of outrageous fortune,
> Or to take arms against a sea of troubles,
> And, by opposing, end them.

And, by contrast, the first quarto version:

> To be, or not to be, I there's the point,
> To Die, to sleep, is that all? I all:

For scholar Henry David Gray the first quarto lines are emblematic of "a distorted version of the completed drama filled out and revised by an inferior poet" and based, he goes on to argue, on the fractured memories of the play as witnessed and performed by the actor playing Marcellus. Gray, and several other critics, consider the first quarto a pirated copy, printed in haste without the writer's permission in an attempt to make quick money following the success of the play in the theatre. In understanding the significance of Marcellus to the theory it is imperative to note that the authenticity of each quarto is based on its similarities to the version of the play found in the first folio, printed in 1623 and believed to be authorised by Shakespeare. Therefore, since in the folio version of *Hamlet* the "to be or not to be" soliloquy is virtually identical to that of the second quarto, it is believed that the second was authored by Shakespeare himself and that the first, by its considerable differences, must therefore be in some way compromised. However, when read in comparison to the folio version, the only character whose lines are almost entirely perfect are those spoken by Marcellus, which, since dramatic practice at the time was for actors to be given only their own lines and three or four word 'cues' based on the lines preceding theirs, suggests that the first quarto is a memorial reconstruction of the play written by the actor who played Marcellus. Having committed his own lines to memory he was able to reproduce them accurately, but was left to fill in the remaining lines and plot from memory which accounts for the truncated and often vastly inferior writing in the first quarto.

According to the remaining cast lists from the period, Shakespeare remained an actor throughout his career as a writer, and it is thought he continued to act after he retired his pen. In 1616 he is recorded in the cast list in Ben Jonson's collected *Works* in the plays *Man in His Humour* 1598) and *Sejanus His Fall* (1603), though some scholars consider his absence from the list of Jonson's *Volpone* evidence that, by 1605, his acting career was nearing its end. Despite this in the First Folio he is listed as one of "the Principle Actors in all these Plays", several of which were only staged after *Volpone*.

By 1604 he had moved again, remaining north of the river, to an area near St. Paul's Cathedral where he rented a fine room amongst fine houses from Christopher Mountjoy, a French hatmaker and Huguenot.

The Anglo-Welsh poet John Davies of Hereford wrote in 1610 that "good Will" tended to play "kingly" roles, suggesting he was still on stage, perhaps now performing the more mature kings such as Lear and Henry VI. There has even been the suggestion that Shakespeare played the ghost of Hamlet's father, though there is little evidence to suggest it.

In 1608 the King's Men purchased the Blackfriars theatre from Henry Evans, and according to Cuthbert Burbage, one of the most highly regarded actors of the time, "placed many players" there "which were Hemings, Condell, Shakespeare, etc." A 1609 lawsuit brought against John Addenbrooke in Stratford on the 7th of June describes Shakespeare as "generosus nuper in curia domini Jacobi" (a gentleman recently at the court of King James) which indicates that by this time he was spending more time in Stratford. A likely cause of this was the bubonic plague, frequent outbreaks of which demanded the equally frequent closing of places of public gathering, principle among which were the theatres. Between May 1603 and February 1610 the theatres were closed for a total of 60 months, meaning there was no acting work and nobody to perform new plays. Though in 1610 Shakespeare returned to Stratford and it is supposed lived with his wife, he made frequent visits to London between 1611-14, being called as a witness in the trial *Bellott v. Mountjoy*, a case addressing concerns about the marriage settlement of Mountjoy's daughter, Mary. In March 1613 he purchased a gatehouse in the former Blackfriars priory, and spent several weeks in the city with his son-in-law John Hall, a physician, married to his daughter Susanna, from November 1614.

No plays are attributed to Shakespeare after 1613, and the last few plays he wrote before this time were in collaboration with other writers, one of whom is likely to be John Fletcher who succeeded him as the house playwright for the King's Men.

In early 1616 his daughter Judith married Thomas Quiney, a vintner and tobacconist. He signed his last will and testament on March 25th, of the same year, and the following day Quiney was ordered to do public penance for having fathered an illegitimate child with a woman named Margaret Wheeler who had died during childbirth which had enabled Quiney to cover up the scandal. This public humiliation would have been embarrassing for Shakespeare and his family.

William Shakespeare died two months later on April 23rd, 1616, survived by his wife and two daughters.

According to his will the bulk of his considerable estate was left to his elder daughter Susanna, with the instruction that she pass it down intact to "the first son of her body". However, though Susanna and Judith had four children between them they all died without progeny, ending Shakespeare's direct lineage. Also in his will was the instruction that his "second best bed" be left to his wife Anne, likely an insult, though the bed was possibly matrimonial and therefore of significant sentimental value.

He was buried two days after his death in the chancel of the Holy Trinity Church in Stratford-Upon-Avon.

The epitaph on the slab which covers his grave includes the following passage,

> Good frend for Iesvs sake forbeare,
> To digg the dvst encloased heare.

> Bleste be ye man yt spares thes stones,
> And cvrst be he yt moves my bones

which, in modern translation, reads

> Good friend, for Jesus's sake forbear,
> To dig the dust enclosed here.
> Blessed be the man that spares these stones,
> And cursed be he that moves my bones.

At some point before 1623 there was a funerary monument erected in his memory on the north wall of Stratford-upon-Avon which features a half-effigy of him writing, and which likens him to Nestor, Socrates and Virgil.

On January 29th, 1741 a white marble memorial statue to him was erected in Poets' Corner in Westminster Abbey.

Though there have been many monuments built around the world in memory of Shakespeare, undoubtedly the greatest memorial of all is the body of work which became the foundation of Western literary canon and an inspiration for every generation.

William Shakespeare – A Concise Bibliography

1589	Comedy of Errors (Comedy)
1590	Henry VI, Part II (History)
	Henry VI, Part III (History)
1591	Henry VI, Part I (History)
1592	Richard III (History)
1593	Taming of the Shrew (Comedy)
	Titus Andronicus (Tragedy)
	Venus and Adonis (Poem)
1594	Rape of Lucrece (Poem)
	Romeo and Juliet (Tragedy)
	Two Gentlemen of Verona (Comedy)
	Love's Labour's Lost (Comedy)
1595	Richard II (History)
	Midsummer Night's Dream (Comedy)
1596	King John (History)
	Merchant of Venice (Comedy)
1597	Henry IV, Part I (History)
	Henry IV, Part II (History)

1598		Passionate Pilgrim (Poem)
		Henry V (History)
		Much Ado about Nothing (Comedy)
1599		Twelfth Night (Comedy)
		As You Like It (Comedy)
		Julius Caesar (Tragedy)
1600		Hamlet (Tragedy)
		Merry Wives of Windsor (Comedy)
1601		Troilus and Cressida (Comedy)
1601		Phoenix and the Turtle (Poem))
1602		All's Well That Ends Well (Comedy)
1604		Othello (Tragedy)
		Measure for Measure
1605		King Lear (Tragedy)
		Macbeth (Tragedy)
1606		Antony and Cleopatra (Tragedy)
1607		Coriolanus (Tragedy)
		Timon of Athens (Tragedy)
1608		Pericles (Comedy)
1609		Cymbeline (Comedy)
		Lover's Complaint (Poem)
1610		Winter's Tale (Comedy)
1611		Tempest (Comedy)
1612		Henry VIII (History)

As regards his 154 sonnets it is almost impossible to date each individually though collectively they were first published in 1609, with two having been published in 1599.

Shakspeare; or, the Poet by Ralph Waldo Emerson

Great (1) men are more distinguished by range and extent than by originality. If we require the originality which consists in weaving, like a spider, their web from their own bowels; in finding clay and making bricks and building the house; no great men are original. Nor does valuable originality consist in unlikeness to other men. The hero is in the press of knights and the thick of events; and seeing what men want and sharing their desire, he adds the needful length of sight and of arm, to come at the desired point. The greatest genius is the most indebted man. A poet is no rattle-brain, saying what comes uppermost, and, because he says every thing, saying at last something good; but a heart in unison with his time and country. There is nothing whimsical and fantastic in his production, but sweet and sad earnest, freighted with the weightiest convictions and pointed with the most determined aim which any man or class knows of in his times. (2)

The Genius of our life is jealous of individuals, and will not have any individual great, except through the general. There is no choice to genius. A great man does not wake up on some fine morning and say, 'I am full of life, I will go to sea and find an Antarctic continent: to-day I will square the circle: I will ransack botany and find a new food for man: I have a new architecture in my mind: I foresee a new mechanic power:' no, but he finds himself in the river of the thoughts and events, forced onward by the ideas and necessities of his contemporaries. (3) He stands where all the eyes of men look one way, and their hands all point in the direction in which he should go. The Church has reared him amidst rites and pomps, and he carries out the advice which her music gave him, and builds a cathedral needed by her chants and processions. He finds a war raging: it educates him, by trumpet, in barracks, and he betters the instruction. He finds two counties groping to bring coal, or flour, or fish, from the place of production to the place of consumption, and he hits on a railroad. Every master has found his materials collected, and his power lay in his sympathy with his people and in his love of the materials he wrought in. What an economy of power! and what a compensation for the shortness of life! All is done to his hand. The world has brought him thus far on his way. The human race has gone out before him, sunk the hills, filled the hollows and bridged the rivers. Men, nations, poets, artisans, women, all have worked for him, and he enters into their labors. Choose any other thing, out of the line of tendency, out of the national feeling and history, and he would have all to do for himself: his powers would be expended in the first preparations. Great genial power, one would almost say, consists in not being original at all; in being altogether receptive; in letting the world do all, and suffering the spirit of the hour to pass unobstructed through the mind. (4)

Shakspeare's youth fell in a time when the English people were importunate for dramatic entertainments. The court took offence easily at political allusions and attempted to suppress them. The Puritans, a growing and energetic party, and the religious among the Anglican church, would suppress them. But the people wanted them. Inn-yards, houses without roofs, and extemporaneous enclosures at country fairs were the ready theatres of strolling players. The people had tasted this new joy; and, as we could not hope to suppress newspapers now,—no, not by the strongest party,—neither then could king, prelate, or puritan, alone or united, suppress an organ which was ballad, epic, newspaper, caucus, lecture, Punch and library, at the same time. Probably king, prelate and puritan, all found their own account in it. It had become, by all causes, a national interest,—by no means conspicuous, so that some great scholar would have thought of treating it in an English history,—but not a whit less considerable because it was cheap and of no account, like a baker's-shop. The best proof of its vitality is the crowd of writers which suddenly broke into this field; Kyd, Marlow, Greene, Jonson, Chapman, Dekker, Webster, Heywood, Middleton, Peele, Ford, Massinger, Beaumont and Fletcher.

The secure possession, by the stage, of the public mind, is of the first importance to the poet who works for it. (5) He loses no time in idle experiments. Here is audience and expectation prepared. In the case of Shakspeare there is much more. At the time when he left Stratford and went up to London, a great body of stage-plays of all dates and writers existed in manuscript and were in turn produced on the boards. Here is the Tale of Troy, which the audience will bear hearing some part of, every week; the Death of Julius Cæsar, and other stories out of Plutarch, which they never tire of; a shelf full of English history, from the chronicles of Brut and Arthur, down to the royal Henries, which men hear eagerly; and a string of doleful tragedies, merry Italian tales and Spanish voyages, which all the London 'prentices know. All the mass has been treated, with more or less skill, by every playwright, and the prompter has the soiled and tattered manuscripts. It is now no longer possible to say who wrote them first. They have been the property of the Theatre so long, and so many rising geniuses have enlarged or altered them, inserting a speech or a whole scene, or adding a song, that no man can any longer claim copyright in this work of numbers. Happily, no man wishes to. They are not yet desired in that way. We have few readers, many spectators and hearers. They had best lie where they are.

Shakspeare, in common with his comrades, esteemed the mass of old plays waste stock, in which any experiment could be freely tried. Had the prestige which hedges about a modern tragedy existed, nothing could have been done. The rude warm blood of the living England circulated in the play, as in street-ballads, and gave body which he wanted to his airy and majestic fancy. The poet needs a ground in popular tradition on which he may work, and which, again, may restrain his art within the due temperance. It holds him to the people, supplies a foundation for his edifice, and in furnishing so much work done to his hand, leaves him at leisure and in full strength for the audacities of his imagination. In short, the poet owes to his legend what sculpture owed to the temple. Sculpture in Egypt and in Greece grew up in subordination to architecture. It was the ornament of the temple wall: at first a rude relief carved on pediments, then the relief became bolder and a head or arm was projected from the wall; the groups being still arranged with reference to the building, which serves also as a frame to hold the figures; and when at last the greatest freedom of style and treatment was reached, the prevailing genius of architecture still enforced a certain calmness and continence in the statue. As soon as the statue was begun for itself, and with no reference to the temple or palace, the art began to decline: freak, extravagance and exhibition took the place of the old temperance. This balance-wheel, which the sculptor found in architecture, the perilous irritability of poetic talent found in the accumulated dramatic materials to which the people were already wonted, and which had a certain excellence which no single genius, however extraordinary, could hope to create.

In point of fact it appears that Shakspeare did owe debts in all directions, and was able to use whatever he found; and the amount of indebtedness may be inferred from Malone's laborious computations in regard to the First, Second and Third parts of Henry VI., in which, "out of 6043 lines, 1771 were written by some author preceding Shakspeare, 2373 by him, on the foundation laid by his predecessors, and 1899 were entirely his own." And the proceeding investigation hardly leaves a single drama of his absolute invention. Malone's sentence is an important piece of external history. In Henry VIII. I think I see plainly the cropping out of the original rock on which his own finer stratum was laid. The first play was written by a superior, thoughtful man, with a vicious ear. I can mark his lines, and know well their cadence. See Wolsey's soliloquy, and the following scene with Cromwell, where instead of the metre of Shakspeare, whose secret is that the thought constructs the tune, so that reading for the sense will best bring out the rhythm,—here the lines are constructed on a given tune, and the verse has even a trace of pulpit eloquence. But the play contains through all its length unmistakable traits of Shakspeare's hand, and some passages, as the account of the coronation, are like autographs. What is odd, the compliment to Queen Elizabeth is in the bad rhythm. (6)

Shakspeare knew that tradition supplies a better fable than any invention can. If he lost any credit of design, he augmented his resources; and, at that day, our petulant demand for originality was not so much pressed. There was no literature for the million. The universal reading, the cheap press, were unknown. A great poet who appears in illiterate times, absorbs into his sphere all the light which is any where radiating. Every intellectual jewel, every flower of sentiment it is his fine office to bring to his people; and he comes to value his memory equally with his invention. (7) He is therefore little solicitous whence his thoughts have been derived; whether through translation, whether through tradition, whether by travel in distant countries, whether by inspiration; from whatever source, they are equally welcome to his uncritical audience. Nay, he borrows very near home. Other men say wise things as well as he; only they say a good many foolish things, and do not know when they have spoken wisely. He knows the sparkle of the true stone, and puts it in high place, wherever he finds it. (8) Such is the happy position of Homer perhaps; of Chaucer, of Saadi. They felt that all wit was their wit. And they are librarians and historiographers, as well as poets. Each romancer was heir and dispenser of all the hundred tales of the world,—

"Presenting Thebes' and Pelops' line
And the tale of Troy divine." (9)

The influence of Chaucer is conspicuous in all our early literature; and more recently not only Pope and Dryden have been beholden to him, but, in the whole society of English writers, a large unacknowledged debt is easily traced. One is charmed with the opulence which feeds so many pensioners. But Chaucer is a huge borrower. Chaucer, it seems, drew continually, through Lydgate and Caxton, from Guido di Colonna, whose Latin romance of the Trojan war was in turn a compilation from Dares Phrygius, Ovid and Statius. Then Petrarch, Boccaccio and the Provençal poets are his benefactors: the Romaunt of the Rose is only judicious translation from William of Lorris and John of Meung: Troilus and Creseide, from Lollius of Urbino: The Cock and the Fox, from the Lais of Marie: The House of Fame, from the French or Italian: and poor Gower he uses as if he were only a brick-kiln or stone-quarry out of which to build his house. (10) He steals by this apology,—that what he takes has no worth where he finds it and the greatest where he leaves it. It has come to be practically a sort of rule in literature, that a man having once shown himself capable of original writing, is entitled thenceforth to steal from the writings of others at discretion. Thought is the property of him who can entertain it and of him who can adequately place it. A certain awkwardness marks the use of borrowed thoughts; but as soon as we have learned what to do with them they become our own.

Thus all originality is relative. Every thinker is retrospective. The learned member of the legislature, at Westminster or at Washington, speaks and votes for thousands. Show us the constituency, and the now invisible channels by which the senator is made aware of their wishes; the crowd of practical and knowing men, who, by correspondence or conversation, are feeding him with evidence, anecdotes and estimates, and it will bereave his fine attitude and resistance of something of their impressiveness. As Sir Robert Peel and Mr. Webster vote, so Locke and Rousseau think, for thousands; and so there were fountains all around Homer, (11) Menu, Saadi, or Milton, from which they drew; friends, lovers, books, traditions, proverbs,—all perished—which, if seen, would go to reduce the wonder. Did the bard speak with authority? Did he feel himself overmatched by any companion? The appeal is to the consciousness of the writer. Is there at last in his breast a Delphi whereof to ask concerning any thought or thing, whether it be verily so, yea or nay? and to have answer, and to rely on that? All the debts which such a man could contract to other wit would never disturb his consciousness of originality; for the ministrations of books and of other minds are a whiff of smoke to that most private reality with which he has conversed. (12)

It is easy to see that what is best written or done by genius in the world, was no man's work, but came by wide social labor, when a thousand wrought like one, sharing the same impulse. Our English Bible is a wonderful specimen of the strength and music of the English language. But it was not made by one man, or at one time; but centuries and churches brought it to perfection. There never was a time when there was not some translation existing. The Liturgy, admired for its energy and pathos, is an anthology of the piety of ages and nations, a translation of the prayers and forms of the Catholic church,—these collected, too, in long periods, from the prayers and meditations of every saint and sacred writer all over the world. (13) Grotius makes the like remark in respect to the Lord's Prayer, that the single clauses of which it is composed were already in use in the time of Christ, in the Rabbinical forms. He picked out the grains of gold. The nervous language of the Common Law, the impressive forms of our courts and the precision and substantial truth of the legal distinctions, are the contribution of all the sharp-sighted, strong-minded men who have lived in the countries where these laws govern. The translation of Plutarch gets its excellence by being translation on translation. There never was a time when there was none. All the truly idiomatic and national phrases are kept, and all others successively picked out and thrown away. Something like the same process had gone on, long before, with the originals of these books. The world takes liberties with world-books. Vedas, Æsop's Fables, Pilpay, Arabian Nights, Cid, Iliad, Robin Hood, Scottish Minstrelsy, are not the work of single men. In the composition of such works the time thinks, the market thinks, the mason, the carpenter, the merchant, the farmer, the fop, all think for us. Every book supplies its time with one good word; every municipal law, every trade, every folly of the day; and the generic catholic genius who is not afraid or ashamed to owe his originality to the originality of all, stands with the next age as the recorder and embodiment of his own. (14)

We have to thank the researches of antiquaries, and the Shakspeare Society, for ascertaining the steps of the English drama, from the Mysteries celebrated in churches and by churchmen, and the final detachment from the church, and the completion of secular plays, from Ferrex and Porrex, (15) and Gammer Gurton's Needle, down to the possession of the stage by the very pieces which Shakspeare altered, remodelled and finally made his own. Elated with success and piqued by the growing interest of the problem, they have left no bookstall unsearched, no chest in a garret unopened, no file of old yellow accounts to decompose in damp and worms, so keen was the hope to discover whether the boy Shakspeare poached or not, whether he held horses at the theatre door, whether he kept school, and why he left in his will only his second-best bed to Ann Hathaway, his wife.

There is somewhat touching in the madness with which the passing age mischooses the object on which all candles shine and all eyes are turned; the care with which it registers every trifle touching Queen Elizabeth and King James, and the Essexes, Leicesters, Burleighs and Buckinghams; and lets pass without a single valuable note the founder of another dynasty, which alone will cause the Tudor dynasty to be remembered,—the man who carries the Saxon race in him by the inspiration which feeds him, and on whose thoughts the foremost people of the world are now for some ages to be nourished, and minds to receive this and not another bias. A popular player;—nobody suspected he was the poet of the human race; and the secret was kept as faithfully from poets and intellectual men as from courtiers and frivolous people. (16) Bacon, who took the inventory of the human understanding for his times, never mentioned his name. Ben Jonson, though we have strained his few words of regard and panegyric, had no suspicion of the elastic fame whose first vibrations he was attempting. He no doubt thought the praise he has conceded to him generous, and esteemed himself, out of all question, the better poet of the two.

If it need wit to know wit, according to the proverb, Shakspeare's time should be capable of recognizing it. Sir Henry Wotton was born four years after Shakspeare, and died twenty-three years after him; and I find, among his correspondents and acquaintances, the following persons: Theodore Beza, Isaac Casaubon, Sir Philip Sidney, the Earl of Essex, Lord Bacon, Sir Walter Raleigh, John Milton, Sir Henry Vane, Isaac Walton, Dr. Donne, Abraham Cowley, Bellarmine, Charles Cotton, John Pym, John Hales, Kepler, Vieta, Albericus Gentilis, Paul Sarpi, Arminius; with all of whom exists some token of his having communicated, without enumerating many others whom doubtless he saw,—Shakspeare, Spenser, Jonson, Beaumont, Massinger, the two Herberts, Marlow, Chapman and the rest. Since the constellation of great men who appeared in Greece in the time of Pericles, there was never any such society;—yet their genius failed them to find out the best head in the universe. (17) Our poet's mask was impenetrable. You cannot see the mountain near. It took a century to make it suspected; and not until two centuries had passed, after his death, did any criticism which we think adequate begin to appear. It was not possible to write the history of Shakspeare till now; for he is the father of German literature: it was with the introduction of Shakspeare into German, by Lessing, and the translation of his works by Wieland and Schlegel, that the rapid burst of German literature was most intimately connected. It was not until the nineteenth century, whose speculative genius is a sort of living Hamlet, that the tragedy of Hamlet could find such wondering readers. (18) Now, literature, philosophy and thought are Shakspearized. His mind is the horizon beyond which, at present, we do not see. Our ears are educated to music by his rhythm. Coleridge and Goethe are the only critics who have expressed our convictions with any adequate fidelity: but there is in all cultivated minds a silent appreciation of his superlative power and beauty, which, like Christianity, qualifies the period.

The Shakspeare Society have inquired in all directions, advertised the missing facts, offered money for any information that will lead to proof,—and with what result? Beside some important illustration of the history of the English stage, to which I have adverted, they have gleaned a few facts touching the property, and dealings in regard to property, of the poet. It appears that from year to year he owned a larger share in the Blackfriars' Theatre: its wardrobe and other appurtenances were his: that he bought an estate in his native village with his earnings as writer and shareholder; that he lived in the best house in Stratford; was intrusted by his neighbors with their commissions in London, as of borrowing money, and the like; that he was a veritable farmer. About the time when he was writing Macbeth, he sues Philip Rogers, in the borough-court of Stratford, for thirty-five shillings, ten pence, for corn delivered to him at different times; and in all respects appears as a good husband, with no reputation for eccentricity or excess. He was a good-natured sort of man, an actor and shareholder in the theatre, not in any striking manner distinguished from other actors and managers. (19) I admit the importance of this information. It was well worth the pains that have been taken to procure it.

But whatever scraps of information concerning his condition these researches may have rescued, they can shed no light upon that infinite invention which is the concealed magnet of his attraction for us. We are very clumsy writers of history. We tell the chronicle of parentage, birth, birth-place, schooling, school-mates, earning of money, marriage, publication of books, celebrity, death; and when we have come to an end of this gossip, no ray of relation appears between it and the goddess-born; and it seems as if, had we dipped at random into the "Modern Plutarch," and read any other life there, it would have fitted the poems as well. (20) It is the essence of poetry to spring, like the rainbow daughter of Wonder, from the invisible, to abolish the past and refuse all history. Malone, Warburton, Dyce and Collier have wasted their oil. The famed theatres, Covent Garden, Drury Lane, the Park and Tremont have vainly assisted. Betterton, Garrick, Kemble, Kean and Macready dedicate their lives to this genius; him they crown, elucidate, obey and express. The genius knows them not. The recitation begins; one golden word leaps out immortal from all this painted pedantry and sweetly torments us with invitations to its own inaccessible homes. I remember I went once to see the Hamlet of a famed performer, the pride of the English stage; and all I then heard and all I now remember of the tragedian was that in which the tragedian had no part; simply Hamlet's question to the ghost:—

"What may this mean,
That thou, dead corse, again in complete steel
Revisit'st thus the glimpses of the moon?"

That imagination which dilates the closet he writes in to the world's dimension, crowds it with agents in rank and order, as quickly reduces the big reality to be the glimpses of the moon. (21) These tricks of his magic spoil for us the illusions of the green-room. Can any biography shed light on the localities into which the Midsummer Night's Dream admits me? Did Shakspeare confide to any notary or parish recorder, sacristan, or surrogate in Stratford, the genesis of that delicate creation?

The forest of Arden, the nimble air of Scone Castle, the moonlight of Portia's villa, "the antres vast and desarts idle" of Othello's captivity,—where is the third cousin, or grand-nephew, the chancellor's file of accounts, or private letter, that has kept one word of those transcendent secrets? In fine, in this drama, as in all great works of art,—in the Cyclopæan architecture of Egypt and India, in the Phidian sculpture, the Gothic minsters, the Italian painting, the Ballads of Spain and Scotland,—the Genius draws up the ladder after him, when the creative age goes up to heaven, and gives way to a new age, which sees the works and asks in vain for a history.

Shakspeare is the only biographer of Shakspeare; and even he can tell nothing, except to the Shakspeare in us, that is, to our most apprehensive and sympathetic hour. (22) He cannot step from off his tripod and give us anecdotes of his inspirations. Read the antique documents extricated, analyzed and compared by the assiduous Dyce and Collier, and now read one of these skyey sentences,—aerolites,—which seem to have fallen out of heaven, and which not your experience but the man within the breast has accepted as words of fate, and tell me if they match; if the former account in any manner for the latter; or which gives the most historical insight into the man.

Hence, though our external history is so meagre, yet, with Shakspeare for biographer, instead of Aubrey and Rowe, we have really the information which is material; that which describes character and fortune, that which, if we were about to meet the man and deal with him, would most import us to know. We have his recorded convictions on those questions which knock for answer at every heart,—on life and death, on love, on wealth and poverty, on the prizes of life and the ways whereby we come at them; on the characters of men, and the influences, occult and open, which affect their fortunes; and on those mysterious and demoniacal powers which defy our science and which yet interweave their malice and their gift in our brightest hours. Who ever read the volume of the Sonnets without finding that the poet had there revealed, under masks that are no masks to the intelligent, the lore of friendship and of love; the confusion of sentiments in the most susceptible, and, at the same time, the most intellectual of men? What trait of his private mind has he hidden in his dramas? One can discern, in his ample pictures of the gentleman and the king, what forms and humanities pleased him; his delight in troops of friends, in large hospitality, in cheerful giving. Let Timon, let Warwick, let Antonio the merchant answer for his great heart. So far from Shakspeare's being the least known, he is the one person, in all modern history, known to us. What point of morals, of manners, of economy, of philosophy, of religion, of taste, of the conduct of life, has he not settled? What mystery has not signified his knowledge of? What office, or function, or district of man's work, has he not remembered? What king has he not taught state, as Talma taught Napoleon? What maiden has not found him finer than her delicacy? What lover has he not outloved? What sage has he not outseen? What gentleman has he not instructed in the rudeness of his behavior?

Some able and appreciating critics think no criticism on Shakspeare valuable that does not rest purely on the dramatic merit; that he is falsely judged as poet and philosopher. I think as highly as these critics of his dramatic merit, but still think it secondary. He was a full man, who liked to talk; a brain exhaling thoughts and images, which, seeking vent, found the drama next at hand. (23) Had he been less, we should have had to consider how well he filled his place, how good a dramatist he was,—and he is the best in the world. But it turns out that what he has to say is of that weight as to withdraw some attention from the vehicle; and he is like some saint whose history is to be rendered into all languages, into verse and prose, into songs and pictures, and cut up into proverbs; so that the occasion which gave the saint's meaning the form of a conversation, or of a prayer, or of a code of laws, is immaterial compared with the universality of its application. So it fares with the wise Shakspeare and his book of life. He wrote the airs for all our modern music: he wrote the text of modern life; the text of manners: he drew the man of England and Europe; the father of the man in America; (24) he drew the man, and described the day, and what is done in it: he read the hearts of men and women, their probity, and their second thought and wiles; the wiles of innocence, and the transitions by which virtues and vices slide into their contraries: he could divide the mother's part from the father's part in the face of the child, or draw the fine demarcations of freedom and of fate: he knew the laws of repression which make the police of nature: and all the sweets and all the terrors of human lot lay in his mind as truly but as softly as the landscape lies on the eye. And the importance of this wisdom of life sinks the form, as of Drama or Epic, out of notice. 'T is like making a question concerning the paper on which a king's message is written.

Shakspeare is as much out of the category of eminent authors, as he is out of the crowd. He is inconceivably wise; the others, conceivably. A good reader can, in a sort, nestle into Plato's brain and think from thence; but not into Shakspeare's. We are still out of doors. For executive faculty, for creation, Shakspeare is unique. No man can imagine it better. He was the farthest reach of subtlety compatible with an individual self,—the subtlest of authors, and only just within the possibility of authorship. (25) With this wisdom of life is the equal endowment of imaginative and of lyric power. He clothed the creatures of his legend with form and sentiments as if they were people who had lived under his roof; and few real men have left such distinct characters as these fictions. And they spoke in language as sweet as it was fit. Yet his talents never seduced him into an ostentation, nor did he harp on one string. An omnipresent humanity co-ordinates all his faculties. Give a man of talents a story to tell, and his partiality will presently appear. He has certain observations, opinions, topics, which have some accidental prominence, and which he disposes all to exhibit. He crams this part and starves that other part, consulting not the fitness of the thing, but his fitness and strength. But Shakspeare has no peculiarity, no importunate topic; but all is duly given; no veins, no curiosities; no cow-painter, no bird-fancier, no mannerist is he: he has no discoverable egotism: the great he tells greatly; the small subordinately. He is wise without emphasis or assertion; he is strong, as nature is strong, who lifts the land into mountain slopes without effort and by the same rule as she floats a bubble in the air, and likes as well to do the one as the other. This makes that equality of power in farce, tragedy, narrative, and love-songs; a merit so incessant that each reader is incredulous of the perception of other readers.

This power of expression, or of transferring the inmost truth of things into music and verse, makes him the type of the poet and has added a new problem to metaphysics. This is that which throws him into natural history, as a main production of the globe, and as announcing new eras and ameliorations. Things were mirrored in his poetry without loss or blur: he could paint the fine with precision, the great with compass, the tragic and the comic indifferently and without any distortion or favor. He carried his powerful execution into minute details, to a hair point; finishes an eyelash or a dimple as firmly as he draws a mountain; and yet these, like nature's, will bear the scrutiny of the solar microscope.

In short, he is the chief example to prove that more or less of production, more or fewer pictures, is a thing indifferent. He had the power to make one picture. Daguerre learned how to let one flower etch its image on his plate of iodine, and then proceeds at leisure to etch a million. There are always objects; but there was never representation. Here is perfect representation, at last; and now let the world of figures sit for their portraits. No recipe can be given for the making of a Shakspeare; but the possibility of the translation of things into song is demonstrated.

His lyric power lies in the genius of the piece. The sonnets, though their excellence is lost in the splendor of the dramas, are as inimitable as they; and it is not a merit of lines, but a total merit of the piece; like the tone of voice of some incomparable person, so is this a speech of poetic beings, and any clause as unproducible now as a whole poem.

Though the speeches in the plays, and single lines, have a beauty which tempts the ear to pause on them for their euphuism, yet the sentence is so loaded with meaning and so linked with its foregoers and followers, that the logician is satisfied. His means are as admirable as his ends; every subordinate invention, by which he helps himself to connect some irreconcilable opposites, is a poem too. He is not reduced to dismount and walk because his horses are running off with him in some distant direction: he always rides.

The finest poetry was first experience; but the thought has suffered a transformation since it was an experience. Cultivated men often attain a good degree of skill in writing verses; but it is easy to read, through their poems, their personal history: any one acquainted with the parties can name every figure; this is Andrew and that is Rachel. The sense thus remains prosaic. It is a caterpillar with wings, and not yet a butterfly. In the poet's mind the fact has gone quite over into the new element of thought, and has lost all that is exuvial. This generosity abides with Shakespeare. We say, from the truth and closeness of his pictures, that he knows the lesson by heart. Yet there is not a trace of egotism.

One more royal trait properly belongs to the poet. I mean his cheerfulness, without which no man can be a poet,—for beauty is his aim. He loves virtue, not for its obligation but for its grace: he delights in the world, in man, in woman, for the lovely light that sparkles from them. Beauty, the spirit of joy and hilarity, he sheds over the universe. Epicurus relates that poetry hath such charms that a lover might forsake his mistress to partake of them. And the true bards have been noted for their firm and cheerful temper. Homer lies in sunshine; Chaucer is glad and erect; and Saadi says, "It was rumored abroad that I was penitent; but what had I to do with repentance?" (26) Not less sovereign and cheerful,—much more sovereign and cheerful, is the tone of Shakespeare. His name suggests joy and emancipation to the heart of men. If he should appear in any company of human souls, who would not march in his troop? He touches nothing that does not borrow health and longevity from his festal style.

And now, how stands the account of man with this bard and benefactor, when, in solitude, shutting our ears to the reverberations of his fame, we seek to strike the balance? Solitude has austere lessons; it can teach us to spare both heroes and poets; and it weighs Shakespeare also, and finds him to share the halfness and imperfection of humanity.

Shakespeare, Homer, Dante, Chaucer, saw the splendor of meaning that plays over the visible world; knew that a tree had another use than for apples, and corn another than for meal, and the ball of the earth, than for tillage and roads: that these things bore a second and finer harvest to the mind, being emblems of its thoughts, and conveying in all their natural history a certain mute commentary on human life. (27) Shakespeare employed them as colors to compose his picture. He rested in their beauty; and never took the step which seemed inevitable to such genius, namely to explore the virtue which resides in these symbols and imparts this power:—what is that which they themselves say? He converted the elements which waited on his command, into entertainments. He was master of the revels to mankind. Is it not as if one should have, through majestic powers of science, the comets given into his hand, or the planets and their moons, and should draw them from their orbits to glare with the municipal fireworks on a holiday night, and advertise in all towns, "Very superior pyrotechny this evening"? Are the agents of nature, and the power to understand them, worth no more than a street serenade, or the breath of a cigar? One remembers again the trumpet-text in the Koran,—"The heavens and the earth and all that is between them, think ye we have created them in jest?" As long as the question is of talent and mental power, the world of men has not his equal to show. But when the question is, to life and its materials and its auxiliaries, how does he profit me? What does it signify? It is but a Twelfth Night, or Midsummer-Night's Dream, or Winter Evening's Tale: what signifies another picture more or less? The Egyptian verdict of the Shakespeare Societies comes to mind; that he was a jovial actor and manager. I can not marry this fact to his verse. Other admirable men have led lives in some sort of keeping with their thought; but this man, in wide contrast. Had he been less, had he reached only the common measure of great authors, of Bacon, Milton, Tasso, Cervantes, we might leave the fact in the twilight of human fate: but that this man of men, he who gave to the science of mind a new and larger subject than had ever existed, and planted the standard of humanity some furlongs forward into Chaos,—that he should not be wise for himself;—it must even go into the world's history that the best poet led an obscure and profane life, using his genius for the public amusement. (28)

Well, other men, priest and prophet, Israelite, German and Swede, beheld the same objects: they also saw through them that which was contained. And to what purpose? The beauty straightway vanished; they read commandments, all-excluding mountainous duty; an obligation, a sadness, as of piled mountains, fell on them, and life became ghastly, joyless, a pilgrim's progress, a probation, beleaguered round with doleful histories of Adam's fall and curse behind us; with doomsdays and purgatorial and penal fires before us; and the heart of the seer and the heart of the listener sank in them.

It must be conceded that these are half-views of half-men. The world still wants its poet-priest, a reconciler, who shall not trifle, with Shakespeare the player, nor shall grope in graves, with Swedenborg the mourner; but who shall see, speak, and act, with equal inspiration. For knowledge will brighten the sunshine; right is more beautiful than private affection; and love is compatible with universal wisdom. (29)

Footnotes

Note 1.

This essay was read as a lecture in Exeter Hall, in London, in June, 1848.

Perhaps it is well to bear in mind that Mr. Emerson was reared for the ministry and ordained a clergyman, and that his ancestors for several generations had exercised that office, and moreover that, in New England, up to his day, theatrical representations had been looked at with disfavor by serious and God-fearing people, and the witnessing of such by a minister would, like dancing, have been considered unbecoming indulgence. Although Mr. Emerson emancipated himself from bonds that were merely professional or artificial, he had an inbred distaste for the common amusements of society, feeling that they were unbecoming to a scholar, and that he was not adapted for them, though he was tolerant of them in other people. There was a natural earnestness, and a simple and cheerful asceticism in his early and later life. Yet once in his later life, when he had been induced to go to see Mr. and Mrs. Barney Williams in some bright comedy, he praised their acting and admitted to his daughter that he really much enjoyed theatrical performances, in spite of the feeling that they were not for him. Dancing, for instance, which he considered a proper part of youths' education, would have seemed unbecoming for himself. He says, "It shall be writ in my memoirs ... as it was writ of St. Pachonius, Pes ejus ad saltandum non est commotus omni vita sua." His staying away from theatrical entertainments was instinctive, but he was liberal in the matter and would go to see a real artist. He even went to see the performance of the beautiful dancer Fanny Elssler, although a story which has been too often repeated of his remarks to Margaret Fuller on the subject is as false as it is silly.

In Paris he saw Rachel during the Revolution of 1848, and often told his children of her fierce and splendid declamation of the Marseillaise in the theatre, holding the tricolor aloft. On London in that same year he wrote of seeing Macready in Lear, with Mrs. Butler as Cordelia. It was to see one of

Shakspeare's heroes rendered by some master that he went, and probably he never was inside a theatre twenty times in his life, and, so sensitive was he to bad taste or ranting, that he was usually sorry that had gone.

The rendering of Richard II. (I cannot remember by whom) more than satisfied him, and he liked to recall the actor's tones in reading this play, an especial favorite of his, to his children. Coriolanus and Julius Cæsar too he enjoyed reading to them, and he selected passages from Shakspeare for them and trained them very carefully for their recitation in school.

He saw Edwin Booth in Boston, and met him later at the house of a friend and had some talk with him. Booth later mentioned with pleasure to their host the fact that Mr. Emerson had not once alluded to his profession or performance in their conversation.

Mr. Emerson once defined the cultivated man as "one who can tell you something new and true about Shakspeare." And he read a good omen for our age in Shakspeare's acceptance: "The book only characterizes the reader. Is Shakspeare the delight of the nineteenth century? That fact only shows whereabouts we are in the ecliptic of the soul."

In writing of Great Men in 1838 in his journal, he says:—

"Swedenborg is scarce yet appreciable. Shakspeare has, for the first time, in our time found adequate criticism, if indeed he have yet found it:—Coleridge, Lamb, Schlegel, Goethe, Very, Herder.

"The great facts of history are four or five names, Homer—Phidias—Jesus—Shakspeare. One or two names more I will not add, but see what these names stand for. All civil history and all philosophy consists of endeavours more or less vain to explain these persons."

In the journal for 1843 he writes: "Plato is weak inasmuch as he is literary. Shakspeare is not literary, but the strong earth itself." Yet from another point of view he writes, "Shakspeare and Plato each sufficed for the culture of a nation."

That Shakspeare and Milton should have been born meant much to him and to mankind. "Who saw Milton, who saw Shakspeare, saw them do their best, and utter their whole heart manlike among their contemporaries."

And again, "No man can be named whose mind still acts on the cultivated intellect of England and America with an energy comparable to that of Milton. As a poet, Shakspeare undoubtedly transcends and far surpasses him in his popularity with foreign nations: but Shakspeare is a voice merely: who and what he was that sang, that sings, we know not."

Note 2.

Mr. Emerson said of Nature:—

No ray is dimmed, no atom worn,
My oldest force is good as new,
And the fresh rose on yonder thorn
Gives back the bending heavens in dew;—

and her cheerful lesson for the artist or poet was that he too could forever re-combine the old material into fresh and splendid pictures. He rejoiced that "the poet is permitted to dip his brush into the old paint-pot with which birds, flowers, the human cheek, the living rock, the broad landscape, the ocean and the eternal sky were painted," and turning from the reading of the plays he says: "'T is Shakspeare's fault that the world appears so empty. He has educated you with his painted world, and this real one seems a huckster's-shop." Again as to his true rendering of men's characters, "I value Shakspeare as a metaphysician and admire the unspoken logic which upholds the structure of Iago, Macbeth, Antony and the rest."

Note 3.

Again the ancient doctrine of the Flowing, and the modern onward and upward stream of Evolution.

Note 4.

The passive Master lent his hand
To the vast soul that o'er him planned.
"The Problem," Poems.

Note 5.

The stage was to Shakspeare his opportunity, as the Lyceum was to Emerson.

Note 6.

Henry VIII., Act V., Scene iv.

Note 7.

This estimate of the value of memory to the poet, typified by the Greeks in their making the Muses the daughters of Mnemosyne, is enlarged upon in the Essay on "Memory" in Natural History of Intellect. Mr. Emerson said once, "Of the most romantic fact the memory is more romantic," and he quotes Quintilian as saying, Quantum ingenii, tantum memoriæ.

Note 8.

In a fragment of verse written in Mr. Emerson's journal of 1831 on the yearning of the poet to enrich himself from the Treasury of the Universe, he says:—

And if to me it is not given
To fetch one ingot thence
Of that unfading gold of Heaven
His merchants may dispense,
Yet well I know the royal mine,

And know the sparkle of its ore,
Know Heaven's truth from lies that shine,—

Explored, they teach us to explore.
"Fragments on the Poet," Poems, Appendix.

Note 9.

Milton, "Il Penseroso."

Note 10.

Taine, in his History of English Literature, thus justifies Chaucer's borrowing or rendering:—

"Chaucer was capable of seeking out, in the old common forest of the middle ages, stories and legends, to replant them in his own soil and make them send out new shoots.... He has the right and power of copying and translating because by dint of retouching he impresses ... his original mark. He re-creates what he imitates.... At the distance of a century and a half he has affinity with the poets of Elizabeth by his gallery of pictures."

The dates of Lydgate and Caxton show a mistake as to his use of them. Caxton, following Chaucer, when he introduced the printing-press to England, printed his poems and those of Lydgate, who was younger than Chaucer. In his House of Fame, Chaucer places, in his vision, "on a pillar higher than the rest, Homer and Livy, Dares the Phrygian, Guido Colonna, Geoffrey of Monmouth and the other historians of the war of Troy" [Taine's History of English Literature], a due recognition of his debt for Troylus and Cryseyde. As for Gower, he was Chaucer's exact contemporary and friend, and Chaucer dedicated this poem to him.

Note 11.

Kipling irreverently tells of Homer's borrowings thus:—

"When 'Omer smote 'is bloomin' lyre,
He 'd 'eard men sing by land an' sea;
An' what he thought 'e might require,
'E went an' took—the same as me!"
And says of his humble audience:—

"They knew 'e stole; 'e knew they knowed.
They did n't tell, nor make a fuss,
But winked at 'Omer down the road,
An' 'e winked back—the same as us!"

Note 12.

Dr. Holmes's remark with regard to the preceding page is: "The reason why Emerson has so much to say on this subject of borrowing, especially when treating of Plato and Shakspeare, is obvious enough. He was arguing his own cause—not defending himself," etc. In Letters and Social Aims, Mr. Emerson discusses Quotation and Originality.

Note 13.

Mr. Emerson had tender associations with the Book of Common Prayer. His mother had been brought up in the Episcopal communion, and the prayer-book of her youth was always by her, though after her marriage she attended her husband's church. [In Mr. Cabot's Memoir, vol. ii. p. 572, see Mr. Emerson's letter on his mother's death.]

Note 14.

Landor says of these borrowings of Shakspeare, "He breathed upon dead bodies and brought them to life."

Note 15.

The princes Ferrex and Porrex, brothers and rivals for the ancient British throne, are characters in the tragedy Gorboduc by Norton and Sackville, to which the date 1561 is assigned. Gammer Gurton's Needle is a comedy of the same period.

Note 16.

Journal, 1864. "Shakspeare puts us all out. No theory will account for him. He neglected his works, perchance he did not know their value? Ay, but he did; witness the sonnets. He went into company as a listener, hiding himself, [Greek]; was only remembered by all as a delightful companion."

Note 17.

England's genius filled all measure
Of heart and soul, of strength and pleasure,
Gave to the mind its emperor,
And life was larger than before:
Nor sequent centuries could hit
Orbit and sum of Shakspeare's wit.
The men who lived with him became
Poets, for the air was fame.
"The Solution," Poems.

Note 18.

While writing this, Mr. Emerson was surrounded by persons paralyzed for active life in the common world by the doubts of conscience or entangled in over-fine-spun webs of their intellect. [back]

Note 19.

Journal, 1837. "I either read or inferred to-day in the Westminster Review that Shakspeare was not a popular man in his day. How true and wise. He sat alone and walked alone, a visionary poet, and came with his piece, modest but discerning, to the players, and was too glad to get it received, whilst he was too superior not to see its transcendent claims."

Note 20.

The following is the "Exordium of a lecture on Poetry and Eloquence," given in London in 1848:

"Shakspeare is nothing but a large utterance. We cannot find that anything in his age was more worth telling than anything in ours; nor give any account of his existence, but only the fact that there was a wonderful symbolizer and expresser, who has no rival in the ages, and who has thrown an accidental lustre over his time and subject."

In the lecture on "Works and Days" he wrote, "Shakspeare made his Hamlet as a bird weaves its nest." And in that on "Inspiration" in Letters and Social Aims: "Shakspeare seems to you miraculous, but the wonderful juxtapositions, parallelisms, transfers, which his genius effected, were all to him locked together as links of a chain, and the mode precisely as conceivable and familiar to higher intelligence as the index-making of the literary hack."

Journal, 1838. "Read Lear yesterday and Hamlet to-day with new wonder and mused much on the great Soul in the broad continuous daylight of these poems. Especially I wonder at the perfect reception this wit and immense knowledge of life and intellectual superiority find in us all in connection with our utter incapacity to produce anything like it. The superior tone of Hamlet in all the conversations how perfectly preserved, without any mediocrity, much less any dulness in the other speakers.

"How real the loftiness! an inborn gentleman; and above that, an exalted intellect. What incessant growth and plenitude of thought,—pausing on itself never an instant, and each sally of wit sufficient to save the play. How true then and unerring the earnest of the dialogue, as when Hamlet talks with the Queen. How terrible his discourse! What less can be said of the perfect mastery, as by a superior being, of the conduct of the drama, as the free introduction of this capital advice to the players; the commanding good sense which never retreats except before the Godhead which inspires certain passages—the more I think of it, the more I wonder. I will think nothing impossible to man. No Parthenon, no sculpture, no picture, no architecture can be named beside this. All this is perfectly visible to me and to many,—the wonderful truth and mastery of this work, of these works,—yet for our lives could not I, or any man, or all men, produce anything comparable to one scene in Hamlet or Lear. With all my admiration of this life-like picture, set me to producing a match for it, and I should instantly depart into mouthing rhetoric…. One other fact Shakspeare presents us; that not by books are great poets made. Somewhat—and much, he unquestionably owes to his books; but you could not find in his circumstances the history of his poems. It was made without hands in his invisible world. A mightier magic than any learning, the deep logic of cause and effect he studied: its roots were cast so deep, therefore it flung out its branches so high."

Note 21.

Mr. Edwin P. Whipple, writing in Harper's Monthly in 1882, relates how in a long drive with Mr. Emerson, after a lecture, "The conversation at last drifted to contemporary actors who assumed to personate leading characters in Shakspeare's greatest plays. Had I ever seen an actor who satisfied me when he pretended to be Hamlet or Othello, Lear or Macbeth? Yes, I had seen the elder Booth in these characters. Though not perfect, he approached nearer to perfection than any other actor I knew—

"'Ah,' said Emerson, [after] the three minutes I consumed in eulogizing Booth,… 'I see you are one of the happy mortals who are capable of being carried away by an actor of Shakspeare. Now, whenever I visit the theatre to witness the performance of one of his dramas, I am carried away by the poet. I went last Tuesday to see Macready in Hamlet. I got along very well until he came to the passage:—

"thou, dead corse, again, in complete steel,
Revisit'st thus the glimpses of the moon:"—

and then actor, theatre, all vanished in view of that solving and dissolving imagination, which could reduce this big globe and all it inherits into mere "glimpses of the moon." The play went on, but, absorbed in this one thought of the mighty master, I paid no heed to it.'

"What specially impressed me, as Emerson was speaking, was his glance at our surroundings as he slowly uttered, 'glimpses of the moon,' for here above us was the same moon which must have given birth to Shakspeare's thought…. Afterward, in his lecture on Shakspeare, Emerson made use of the thought suggested in our ride by moonlight. He said, 'That imagination which dilates the closet he writes in to the world's dimensions, crowds it with agents in rank and order, as quickly reduces the big reality to be the "glimpses of the moon."'... In the printed lecture, there is one sentence declaring the absolute insufficiency of any actor, in any theatre, to fix attention on himself while uttering Shakspeare's words, which seems to me the most exquisite statement ever made of the magical suggestiveness of Shakspeare's expression. I have often quoted it, but it will bear quotation again and again, as the best prose sentence ever written on this side of the Atlantic: 'The recitation begins; one golden word leaps out immortal from all this painted pedantry, and sweetly torments us with invitations to its own inaccessible homes.'"

Note 22.

The little Shakspeare in the maiden's heart
Makes Romeo of a ploughboy on his cart;
Opens the eye to Virtue's starlike meed
And gives persuasion to a gentle deed.
"The Enchanter," Poems, Appendix.

Note 23.

And yet perhaps there is some truth in Dr. Richard Garnett's word in his Life of Emerson:

"Emerson is incapable of contemplating Shakspeare with the eye of a dramatic critic."

Just after Mr. Emerson settled in Concord he read with great pleasure Henry Taylor's play Philip van Artevelde, then recently published. He wrote in his journal for 1835:—

"I think Taylor's poem is the best light we have ever had upon the genius of Shakspeare. We have made a miracle of Shakspeare, a haze of light instead of a guiding torch, by accepting unquestioned all the tavern stories about his want of education, and total unconsciousness. The internal evidence all the time is irresistible that he was no such person. He was a man, like this Taylor, of strong sense and of great cultivation; an excellent Latin scholar, and of extensive and select reading, so as to have formed his theories of many historical characters with as much clearness as Gibbon or Niebuhr or Goethe. He wrote for intelligent persons, and wrote with intention. He had Taylor's strong good sense, and added to it his own wonderful facility of execution which aerates and sublimes all language the moment he uses it, or more truly, animates every word."

Note 24.

Lowell, in one of his essays, calls attention to the survival in New England of the type of face of the English in Queen Elizabeth's day even more than in the mother country, and also to the old English expressions, obsolete in England, but still current on New England farms.

Note 25.

Journal, 1838. fills us with wonder the first time we approach him. We go away, and work and think, for years, and come again,—he astonishes us anew. Then, having drank deeply and saturated us with his genius, we lose sight of him for another period of years. By and by we return, and there he stands immeasurable as at first. We have grown wiser, but only that we should see him wiser than ever. He resembles a high mountain which the traveller sees in the morning, and thinks he shall quickly near it and pass it, and leave it behind. But he journeys all day till noon, till night. There still is the dim mountain close by him, having scarce altered its bearings since the morning light."

Note 26.

And yet it seemeth not to me
That the high gods love tragedy;
For Saadi sat in the sun,
And thanks was his contrition;

And yet his runes he rightly read,
And to his folk his message sped.
"Saadi," Poems.

Note 27.

This image appears in "The Apology" in the Poems.

Note 28.

The Puritan shrinking from the form in which the great poet embodied his thought or oracles or dreams still appears in the journal of 1852, yet, contrasted to the dismal seers, Shakspeare is well-nigh pardoned his levity.

"There was never anything more excellent came from a human brain than the plays of Shakspeare, bating only that they were plays. The Greek has a real advantage of them in the degree in which his dramas had a religious office. Could the priest look him in the face without blenching?"

In 1839 Mr. Emerson had written:—

"It is in the nature of things that the highest originality must be moral. The only person who can be entirely independent of this fountain of literature and equal to it, must be a prophet in his own proper person. Shakspeare, the first literary genius of the world, leans on the Bible: his poetry supposes it. If we examine this brilliant influence, Shakspeare, as it lies in our minds, we shall find it reverent, deeply indebted to the traditional morality, in short, compared with the tone of the prophets, Secondary. On the other hand, the Prophets do not imply the existence of Shakspeare or Homer,—to no books or arts,—only to dread Ideas and emotions."

Note 29.

All through his life Mr. Emerson felt increasing thankfulness for "the Spirit of joy which Shakspeare had shed over the Universe." In 1864 he wrote:—

"When I read Shakspeare, as lately, I think the criticism and study of him to be in their infancy. The wonder grows of his long obscurity:—how could you hide the only man that ever wrote from all men who delight in reading?"

And again he wrote: "Your criticism is profane. Shakspeare by Shakspeare. The poet in his interlunation is a critic,"—that is, his worst is criticised by his best performance.

Journal, 1864. "How to say it I know not, but I know that the point of praise of Shakspeare is the pure poetic power: he is the chosen closet companion, who can, at any moment, by incessant surprises, work the miracle of mythologizing every fact of the common life; as snow, or moonlight, or the level rays of sunrise lend a momentary glow to Pump and wood-pile."

And again: *1836.* "It is easy to solve the problem of individual existence. Why Milton, Shakspeare, or Canova should be there is reason enough. But why the million should exist drunk with the opium of Time and Custom does not appear."

But even Shakspeare must not be idolized. The soul must rely on itself, that is, on the universal fountain of beauty, wisdom and goodness to which it is open. So thus he draws the moral:—

1838. "The indisposition of men to go back to the source and mix with Deity is the reason of degradation and decay. Education is expended in the measurement and imitation of effects in the study of Shakspeare, for example, as itself a perfect being—instead of using Shakspeare merely as an effect of which the cause is with every scholar. Thus the college becomes idolatrous—a temple full of idols. Shakspeare will never be made by the study of Shakspeare. I know not how directions for greatness can be given, yet greatness may be inspired."

Feb. 1838. "Consider too how Shakspeare and Milton are formed. They are just such men as we all are to contemporaries, and none suspected their superiority,—but after all were dead, and a generation or two besides, it is discovered that they surpass all. Each of us then take the same moral to himself."

William Shakespeare – A Tribute in Verse

Index of Contents

To the Memory of My Beloved, the Author, Mr William Shakespeare, & What He Hath Left Us by Ben Jonson
Shakespeare by Matthew Arnold
An Epitaph On The Admirable Dramatic Poet W. Shakespeare by John Milton
Shakespeare by Henry Wadsworth Longfellow
Elegy On Mr. William Shakespeare by William Basse
Shakespeare by Vachel Lindsay
The Spirit of Shakespeare by George Meredith
To Shakespeare by Lord Alfred Douglas
To Shakespeare (I) by Frances Anne Kemble
To Shakespeare (II) by Frances Anne Kemble
To Shakespeare (III) by Frances Anne Kemble
Shakespeare and Milton by Walter Savage Landor
A Shakespeare Memorial by Alfred Austin
Shakespeare by Mathilde Blind
Shakespeare by Robert Crawford
Shakespeare by Thomas Gent
Shakespeare's Mourners by John Bannister Tabb
Shakespeare by Philip Henry Savage
Shakespeare by Lucretia Maria Davidson
Shakespeare by Frederick George Scott
Shakespeare's Kingdom by Alfred Noyes

Shakespeare 1916 by Sir Ronald Ross
Song, In Imitation of Shakspeare's by James Beattie
In A Letter To C. P. Esq. In Imitation o Shakspeare by William Cowper
Shakspeare. (An Ode For His Three-Hundredth Birthday) by Martin Farquhar Tupper
On The Site of A Mulberry-Tree; Planted By Wm. Shakspeare; Felled By The Rev. F. Gastrell by Dante Gabriel Rossetti

To The Memory of My Beloved, The Author, Mr William Shakespeare, And What He Hath Left Us by Ben Jonson

To draw no envy, Shakespeare, on thy name
Am I thus ample to thy book and fame;
While I confess thy writings to be such
As neither Man nor Muse can praise too much.
'Tis true, and all men's suffrage. But these ways
Were not the paths I meant unto thy praise;
For silliest ignorance on these may light,
Which when it sounds at best but echoes right;
Or blind affection, which doth ne'er advance
The truth, but gropes, and urges all by chance;
Or crafty malice might pretend this praise,
And think to ruin where it seemed to raise.
These are as some infamous bawd or whore
Should praise a matron. What could hurt her more?
But thou art proof against them, and indeed
Above th' ill fortune of them, or the need.
I therefore will begin: Soul of the Age!
The applause, delight, the wonder of our stage!
My Shakespeare, rise; I will not lodge thee by
Chaucer, or Spenser, or bid Beaumont lie
A little further, to make thee a room:
Thou art a monument without a tomb,
And art alive still, while thy book doth live,
And we have wits to read, and praise to give.
That I not mix thee so, my brain excuses,
I mean with great but disproportioned Muses,
For if I thought my judgement were of years,
I should commit thee surely with thy peers,
And tell how far thou didst our Lyly outshine,
Or sporting Kyd, or Marlowe's mighty line.
And though thou hadst small Latin and less Greek,
From thence to honour thee I would not seek
For names; but call forth thundering Aeschylus,
Euripides, and Sophocles to us,
Pacuvius, Accius, him of Cordova dead,
To live again, to hear thy buskin tread,
And shake a stage; or, when thy socks were on,
Leave thee alone for the comparison
Of all that insolent Greece or haughty Rome

Sent forth, or since did from their ashes come.
Triumph, my Britain, thou hast one to show
To whom all scenes of Europe homage owe.
He was not of an age, but for all time!
And all the Muses still were in their prime
When, like Apollo, he came forth to warm
Our ears, or, like a Mercury, to charm!
Nature herself was proud of his designs,
And joyed to wear the dressing of his lines!
Which were so richly spun, and woven so fit,
As, since, she will vouchsafe no other wit.
The merry Greek, tart Aristophanes,
Neat Terence, witty Plautus, now not please;
But antiquated and deserted lie,
As they were not of Nature's family.
Yet must I not give Nature all; thy art,
My gentle Shakespeare, must enjoy a part.
For though the poet's matter nature be,
His art doth give the fashion; and that he
Who casts to write a living line must sweat
(Such as thine are) and strike the second heat
Upon the Muses' anvil; turn the same,
And himself with it, that he thinks to frame,
Or for the laurel he may gain a scorn;
For a good poet's made as well as born.
And such wert thou. Look how the father's face
Lives in his issue, even so the race
Of Shakespeare's mind and manners brightly shines
In his well turned and true-filed lines:
In each of which he seems to shake a lance,
As brandished at the eyes of ignorance.
Sweet swan of Avon! what a sight it were
To see thee in our waters yet appear,
And make those flights upon the banks of Thames,
That did so take Eliza and our James!
But stay, I see thee in the hemisphere
Advanced, and made a constellation there:
Shine forth, thou Star of Poets, and with rage,
Or influence, chide or cheer the drooping stage,
Which, since thy flight from hence, hath mourned like night,
And despairs day, but for thy volume's light.

Shakespeare by Matthew Arnold

Others abide our question. Thou art free.
We ask and ask—Thou smilest and art still,
Out-topping knowledge. For the loftiest hill,
Who to the stars uncrowns his majesty,

Planting his steadfast footsteps in the sea,
Making the heaven of heavens his dwelling-place,
Spares but the cloudy border of his base
To the foil'd searching of mortality;

And thou, who didst the stars and sunbeams know,
Self-school'd, self-scann'd, self-honour'd, self-secure,
Didst tread on earth unguess'd at.—Better so!

All pains the immortal spirit must endure,
All weakness which impairs, all griefs which bow,
Find their sole speech in that victorious brow

An Epitaph On The Admirable Dramatic Poet W. Shakespeare by John Milton

What needs my Shakespeare for his honored bones
The labor of an age in piled stones?
Or that his hallowed reliques should be hid
Under a star-ypointing pyramid?
Dear son of Memory, great heir of Fame,
What need'st thou such weak witness of thy name?
Thou in our wonder and astonishment
Hast built thy self a livelong monument.
For whilst, to th' shame of slow-endeavoring art,
Thy easy numbers flow, and that each heart
Hath from the leaves of thy unvalued book
Those Delphic lines with deep impression took,
Then thou, our fancy of itself bereaving,
Dost make us marble with too much conceiving,
And so sepulchred in such pomp dost lie
That kings for such a tomb would wish to die.

Shakespeare by Henry Wadsworth Longfellow

A vision as of crowded city streets,
With human life in endless overflow;
Thunder of thoroughfares; trumpets that blow
To battle; clamor, in obscure retreats,
Of sailors landed from their anchored fleets;
Tolling of bells in turrets, and below
Voices of children, and bright flowers that throw
O'er garden-walls their intermingled sweets!
This vision comes to me when I unfold
The volume of the Poet paramount,
Whom all the Muses loved, not one alone;—
Into his hands they put the lyre of gold,
And, crowned with sacred laurel at their fount,

Placed him as Musagetes on their throne.

Elegy On Mr. William Shakespeare by William Basse

Renowned Spenser, lie a thought more nigh
To learned Chaucer, and rare Beaumont lie
A little nearer Spenser, to make room
For Shakespeare in your threefold, fourfold tomb.
To lodge all four in one bed, make a shift
Until Doomsday, for hardly will a fift
Betwixt this day and that by Fate be slain,
For whom your curtains may be drawn again.
If your precedency in death doth bar
A fourth place in your sacred sepulchre,
Under this carved marble of thine own,
Sleep, rare tragedian, Shakespeare, sleep alone;
Thy unmolested peace, unshared cave
Possess as lord, not tenant of thy grave,
That unto us and others it may be
Honour hereafter to be laid by thee.

Shakespeare by Vachel Lindsay

Would that in body and spirit Shakespeare came
Visible emperor of the deeds of Time,
With Justice still the genius of his rhyme,
Giving each man his due, each passion grace,
Impartial as the rain from Heaven's face
Or sunshine from the heaven-enthroned sun.
Sweet Swan of Avon, come to us again.
Teach us to write, and writing, to be men.

The Spirit of Shakespeare by George Meredith

Thy greatest knew thee, Mother Earth; unsoured
He knew thy sons. He probed from hell to hell
Of human passions, but of love deflowered
His wisdom was not, for he knew thee well.
Thence came the honeyed corner at his lips,
The conquering smile wherein his spirit sails
Calm as the God who the white sea-wave whips,
Yet full of speech and intershifting tales,
Close mirrors of us: thence had he the laugh
We feel is thine: broad as ten thousand beeves
At pasture! thence thy songs, that winnow chaff

From grain, bid sick Philosophy's last leaves
Whirl, if they have no response-they enforced
To fatten Earth when from her soul divorced.

To Shakespeare by Lord Alfred Douglas

Most tuneful singer, lover tenderest,
Most sad, most piteous, and most musical,
Thine is the shrine more pilgrim-worn than all
The shrines of singers; high above the rest
Thy trumpet sounds most loud, most manifest.
Yet better were it if a lonely call
Of woodland birds, a song, a madrigal,
Were all the jetsam of thy sea's unrest.

For now thy praises have become too loud
On vulgar lips, and every yelping cur
Yaps thee a paean; the whiles little men,
Not tall enough to worship in a crowd,
Spit their small wits at thee. Ah! better then
The broken shrine, the lonely worshipper.

To Shakespeare (I) by Frances Anne Kemble

If from the height of that celestial sphere
Where now thou dwell'st, spirit powerful and sweet!
Thou yet canst love the race that sojourn here,
How must thou joy, with pleasure not unmeet
For thy exalted state, to know how dear
Thy memory is held throughout the earth,
Beyond the favoured land that gave thee birth.
E'en in thy seat in Heaven, thou may'st receive
Thanks, praise, and love, and wonder ever new,
From human hearts, who in thy verse perceive
All that humanity calls good and true;
Nor dost thou for each mortal blemish grieve,
They from thy glorious works have fall'n away,
As from thy soul its outward form of clay.

To Shakespeare (II) by Frances Anne Kemble

Oft, when my lips I open to rehearse
Thy wondrous spells of wisdom and of power,
And that my voice and thy immortal verse
On listening ears and hearts I mingled pour,

I shrink dismayed—and awful doth appear
The vain presumption of my own weak deed;
Thy glorious spirit seems to mine so near,
That suddenly I tremble as I read—
Thee an invisible auditor I fear:
Oh, if it might be so, my master dear!
With what beseeching would I pray to thee,
To make me equal to my noble task,
Succour from thee, how humbly would I ask,
Thy worthiest works to utter worthily.

To Shakespeare (III) by Frances Anne Kemble

Shelter and succour such as common men
Afford the weaker partners of their fate,
Have I derived from thee—from thee, most great
And powerful genius! whose sublime control,
Still from thy grave governs each human soul,
That reads the wondrous records of thy pen.
From sordid sorrows thou hast set me free,
And turned from want's grim ways my tottering feet,
And to sad empty hours, given royally,
A labour, than all leisure far more sweet:
The daily bread, for which we humbly pray,
Thou gavest me as if I were thy child,
And still with converse noble, wise, and mild,
Charmed from despair my sinking soul away;
Shall I not bless the need, to which was given
Of all the angels in the host of heaven,
Thee, for my guardian, spirit strong and bland!
Lord of the speech of my dear native land!

Shakespeare and Milton by Walter Savage Landor

The tongue of England, that which myriads
Have spoken and will speak, were paralyz'd
Hereafter, but two mighty men stand forth
Above the flight of ages, two alone;
One crying out,
All nations spoke through me.
The other:
True; and through this trumpet burst God's word;
The fall of Angels, and the doom
First of immortal, then of mortal, Man.
Glory! be glory! not to me, to God.

A Shakespeare Memorial by Alfred Austin

Why should we lodge in marble or in bronze
Spirits more vast than earth, or sea, or sky?
Wiser the silent worshipper that cons
Their words for wisdom that will never die.
Unto the favourite of the passing hour
Erect the statue and parade the bust;
Whereon decisive Time will slowly shower
Oblivion's refuse and disdainful dust.
The Monarchs of the Mind, self-sceptred Kings,
Need no memento to transmit their name:
Throned on their thoughts and high imaginings,
They are the Lords, not sycophants of Fame.
Raise pedestals to perishable stuff:
Gods for themselves are monuments enough.

Shakespeare by Mathilde Blind

Yearning to know herself for all she was,
Her passionate clash of warring good and ill,
Her new life ever ground in Death's old mill,
With every delicate detail and en masse,—
Blind Nature strove. Lo, then it came to pass,
That Time, to work out her unconscious Will,
Once wrought the Mind which she had groped for still,
And she beheld herself as in a glass.

The world of men, unrolled before our sight,
Showed like a map, where stream and waterfall
And village-cradling vale and cloud-capped height
Stand faithfully recorded, great and small;
For Shakespeare was, and at his touch, with light
Impartial as the Sun's, revealed the All.

Shakespeare by Robert Crawford

And what think ye of Shakespeare? 'Twas not he
Of Stratford is the lord of England's lyre;
Ay, not the rustic lad, whoe'er it be,
Momentous in his doing and desire.
But little Latin and less Greek? Ah, no!
It was a teeming scholar who enwrought
The wondrous pages where the wisest go
For th' culmination of the life of thought.
No jovial actor, no mere Shakescene who

Found it so hard his dear name to indite,
The marvellous pictures of our nature drew
And limned the universe in his delight.
We do not know the man; but 'twas not Will
Whose hand is on the lyre of England still.

Shakespeare by Thomas Gent

While o'er this pageant of sublunar things
Oblivion spreads her unrelenting wings,
And sweeps adown her dark unebbing tide
Man, and his mightiest monuments of pride-
Alone, aloft, immutable, sublime,
Star-like, ensphered above the track of time,
Great SHAKSPEARE beams with undiminish'd ray.
His bright creations sacred from decay,
Like Nature's self, whose living form he drew,
Though still the same, still beautiful and new.

He came, untaught in academic bowers,
A gift to Glory from the Sylvan powers:
But what keen Sage, with all the science fraught,
By elder bards or later critics taught,
Shall count the cords of his mellifluous shell,
Span the vast fabric of his fame, and tell
By what strange arts he bade the structure rise-
On what deep site the strong foundation lies?
This, why should scholiasts labour to reveal?
We all can answer it, we all can feel,
Ten thousand sympathies, attesting, start-
For SHAKSPEARE'S Temple, is the human heart!

Lord of a throne which mortal ne'er shall share-
Despot adored! he rales and revels there.
Who but has found, where'er his track hath been,
Through life's oft shifting, multifarious scene,
Still at his side the genial Bard attend,
His loved companion, counsellor, and friend!

The Thespian Sisters nurtured in the schools
Of Greece and Rome, and long coerced by rules,
Scarce moved the inmates of their native hearth
With tiny pathos and with trivial mirth,
Till She, great muse of daring enterprise,
Delighted ENGLAND! saw her SHAKSPEARE rise!

Then, first aroused in that appointed hour,
The Tragic Muse confess'd th' inspiring power;
Sudden before the startled earth she stood,

A giant spectre, weeping tears and blood;
Guilt shrunk appall'd, Despair embraced his shroud,
And Terror shriek'd, and Pity sobb'd aloud;-
Then, first Thalia with dilated ken
And quicken'd footstep pierced the walks of men;
Then Folly blush'd, Vice fled the general hiss,
Delight met Reason with a loving kiss;
At Satire's glance Pride smooth'd his low'ring crest,
The Graces weaved the dance.-And last and best
Came Momus down in Falstaff's form to earth.
To make the world one universe of mirth!

Such Sympathies the glorious Bard endear!
Thus fair he walks in Man's diurnal sphere.
But when, upborne on bright Invention's wings.
He dares the realms of uncreated things,
Forms more divine, more dreadful, start to view,
Than ever Hades or Olympus knew.
Round the dark cauldron, terrible and fell,
The midnight Witches breathe the songs of hell;
Delighted Ariel wings his fiery way
To whirl the storm, the wheeling Orbs to stay;
Then bathes in honey-dews, and sleeps in flowers;
Meanwhile, young Oberon, girt with shadowy powers,
Pursues o'er Ocean's verge the pale cold Moon,
Or hymns her, riding in her highest noon.

Thus graced, thus glorified, shall SHAKSPEARE crave
The Sculptor's skill, the pageant of the grave?
HE needs it not-but Gratitude demands
This votive offering at his Country's hands.
Haply, e'er now, from blissful bowers on high,
From some Parnassus of the empyreal sky,
Pleased, o'er this dome the gentle Spirit bends,
Accepts the gift, and hails us as his friends-
Yet smiles, perchance, to think when envious Time
O'er Bust and Urn shall bid his ivies climb,
When Palaces and Pyramids shall fall-
HIS PAGE SHALL TRIUMPH-still surviving all-
'Till Earth itself, 'like breath upon the wind,'
Shall melt away, 'nor leave a rack behind!'

Shakespeare's Mourners by John Bannister Tabb

I saw the grave of Shakespeare in a dream,
And round about it grouped a wondrous throng,
His own majestic mourners, who belong
Forever to the Stage of Life, and seem
The rivals of reality. Supreme

Stood Hamlet, as erewhile the graves among,
Mantled in thought: and sad Ophelia sung
The same swan-dirge she chanted in the stream.
Othello, dark in destiny's eclipse,
Laid on the tomb a lily. Near him wept
Dejected Constance. Fair Cordelia's lips
Moved prayerfully the while her father slept,
And each and all, inspired of vital breath,
Kept vigil o'er the sacred spoils of death.

Shakespeare by Philip Henry Savage

Through time untimed, if truly great, a Name
Reverence compels and, that forgotten, shame.
But in the stress of living you shall scan,
Yea, touch and censure, great or small, the Man.

Shakespeare by Lucretia Maria Davidson

Shakspeare!' with all thy faults, (and few have more,)
I love thee still,' and still will con thee o'er.
Heaven, in compassion to man's erring heart,
Gave thee of virtue — then, of vice a part,
Lest we, in wonder here, should bow before thee,
Break God's commandment, worship, and adore thee:
But admiration now, and sorrow join;
His works we reverence, while we pity thine.

Shakespeare by Frederick George Scott

Unseen in the great minister dome of time,
Whose shafts are centuries, its spangled roof
The vaulted universe, our master sits,
And organ-voices like a far-off chime
Roll thro' the aisles of thought. The sunlight flits

From arch to arch, and, as he sits aloof,
Kings, heroes, priests, in concourse vast, sublime,
Glances of love and cries from battle-field,
His wizard power breathes on the living air.
Warm faces gleam and pass, child, woman, man,

In the long multitude; but he, concealed,
Our bard eludes us, vainly each face we scan,
It is not he; his features are not there;

But, being thus hid, his greatness is revealed.

Shakespeare's Kingdom by Alfred Noyes

When Shakespeare came to London
He met no shouting throngs;
He carried in his knapsack
A scroll of quiet songs.

No proud heraldic trumpet
Acclaimed him on his way;
Their court and camp have perished;
The songs live on for ay.

Nobody saw or heard them,
But, all around him there,
Spirits of light and music
Went treading the April air.

He passed like any pedlar,
Yet he had wealth untold.
The galleons of th' armada
Could not contain his gold.

The kings rode on to darkness.
In England's conquering hour,
Unseen arrived her splendour;
Unknown, her conquering power.

Shakespeare 1916 by Sir Ronald Ross

Now when the sinking Sun reeketh with blood,
And the gore-gushing vapors rent by him
Rend him and bury him: now the World is dim
As when great thunders gather for the flood,
And in the darkness men die where they stood,
And dying slay, or scatter'd limb from limb
Cease in a flash where mad-eyed cherubim
Of Death destroy them in the night and mud:
When landmarks vanish—murder is become
A glory—cowardice, conscience— and to lie,
A law—to govern, but to serve a time:—
We dying, lifting bloodied eyes and dumb,
Behold the silver star serene on high,
That is thy spirit there, O Master Mind sublime.

Song, In Imitation of Shakspeare's by James Beattie

I
Blow, blow, thou vernal gale!
Thy balm will not avail
To ease my aching breast;
Though thou the billows smooth,
Thy murmurs cannot soothe
My weary soul to rest.

II
Flow, flow, thou tuneful stream!
Infuse the easy dream
Into the peaceful soul;
But thou canst not compose
The tumult of my woes,
Though soft thy waters roll.

III
Blush, blush, ye fairest flowers!
Beauties surpassing yours
My Rosalind adorn;
Nor is the Winter's blast,
That lays your glories waste,
So killing as her scorn.

IV
Breathe, breathe, ye tender lays,
That linger down the maze
Of yonder winding grove;
O let your soft control
Bend her relenting soul
To pity and to love.

V
Fade, fade, ye flowerets fair!
Gales, fan no more the air!
Ye streams, forget to glide;
Be hush'd each vernal strain;
Since nought can soothe my pain,
Nor mitigate her pride.

In A Letter To C. P. Esq. In Imitation Of Shakspeare by William Cowper

Trust me the meed of praise, dealt thriftily
From the nice scale of judgement, honours more
Than does the lavish and o'erbearing tide
Of profuse courtesy. Not all the gems

Of India's richest soil at random spread
O'er the gay vesture of some glittering dame,
Give such alluring vantage to the person,
As the scant lustre of a few, with choice
And comely guise of ornament disposed.

Shakspeare. (An Ode For His Three-Hundredth Birthday) by Martin Farquhar Tupper

I.
Immortal! risen to thy Rest,
Immortal! throned among the Blest,
Immortal! long an heir sublime
Of realms outreaching space and time,—
How shall we dare, or hope, to raise
A fitting homage of high praise
To please thy Spirit, sphered on high
Where planets roll and comets fly?
How may not thy pure fame be marr'd
By the damp breath of earthly bard,
Presuming in his zeal too bold
To gild the bright refinèd gold?
Or how canst thou, fill'd with God's love,
And tranced among the saints above,
Endure that men should seem and be
Idolaters in praise of thee!
Forgive our love, forgive our zeal,—
We cannot guess how spirits feel;
And may our homage offered thus
Please HIM who made both thee, and us!

II.
Immortal also on this darker Earth
As in those brighter spheres,
Now will we consecrate our Shakespeare's birth,
This day three hundred years!
And so from age to age for evermore
His glory shall extend,
With men of every land the wide world o'er,
Till Time itself shall end!
For, he is our's; and well with pride and joy
England may bless her son,
The Stratford scholar and the Warwick boy
That every crown hath won!
Let others boast their wisest and their best,
To each a prize may fall;
Genius gives one apiece to all the rest,
But Shakspeare claims them all!

III.

A Homer, in majestic eloquence,
A Terence, for keen wit and stinging sense,
Brighter than Pindar in his loftiest flight,
Darker than Æschylus for deeds of night,
An Ovid, in the story-pictured page,
A Juvenal, to lash the vicious age,
Graceful as Horace and more skill'd to please,
Tender as pity-stirring Sophocles,
Free as Anacreon, as Martial neat,
Than Virgil's self more delicately sweet,—
O let those ancients bend before Thee now,
And pile their many chaplets on one brow!—
Milton was great, and of divinest song,
Spenser melodious, Chaucer rough and strong,—
The vigorous Dryden, and the classic Gray,
And awful Danté, soaring far away,
Schiller and Göethe, stirring up the strife,
And Molière, dropping laughter into life,
Burns, a full spring of nature, Hood of wit,
And Tennyson, most rare and exquisite,
To each and all belongs the laurell'd crown,
And woe to him who drags their honours down,—
Yet, Shakspeare, thou wert all these lights combined,
O manysided crystal of mankind!

IV.
The jealous Moor, the thoughtful Dane,
The witty rare fat knight,
And grand old Lear half-insane,
And fell Iago's spite,
And Romeo's love, and Tybalt's hate,
And Bolinbroke in regal state,
And he that murdered sleep,—
And ruthless Shylock's bloody bond,
And Prosper with his broken wand
Long buried fathoms deep!
Frank Juliet too,— and that soft pair
Helen and Hermia, lilies fair
As growing on one stem,
Love-crazed Ophelia, drown'd ah! drown'd,
And wanton Cleopatra, crown'd
With Egypt's diadem;
The young Miranda most admired,
Cordelia's filial heart,
Sly Beatrice with wit inspired,
And Ariel's tricksey part,
Fair Rosalind,— sweet banishèd,
And gentle Desdemona — dead!—
Ay these, all these, and crowds beside,
Heroes, jesters, courtiers, clowns,
Girls in grief, or kings in pride,

Threats and crimes, and jokes, and frowns,
Witches, fairies, ghosts, and elves,
All our fancies, all ourselves,—
O! thou hast pictured with thy pen
All phases of all hearts of men,
And in thy various page survives
The Panorama of our lives!

V.
O Paragon unthought before,
O miracle of selftaught lore,
A universe of wit and worth,
The admirable Man of earth,
There is nor thing, nor thought, nor whim,
Untouch'd and unadorn'd by him;
No theme unsung, no truth untold
Of Earth's museum, new or old:
All Nature's hidden things he saw,
Intuitive to every law;
Glancing with supernal scan
At all the knowledge spelt by man;
While, for each rule and craft of Art
He grasp'd it amply, whole and part:
Like travel-wise Ulysses well he knew
Peoples and cities, men and manners too;
With shrewd but ever charitable ken
He read, and wrote out fair, the hearts of men;
Yet, in self-knowledge vers'd, a sage outright,
His giant soul was humble in its might!
O gentle, happy, modest mind,
O genial, cheerful, frank and kind,
Not even could domestic strife
Sour the sweetness of thy life,—
But wheresoe'er thy foot might roam,
Divorced from that Xantipp'd home,
Friends ever found thee,— ay, and foes,
Cordial to these, and kind to those;
Brave, loving, patient, generous, just, and good,—
Beloved by all, our matchless Shakspeare stood!

VI.
Where are thy glorious works unknown?
Who hath not heard thy fame?
On every shore, in every zone,
The World, with glad acclaim,
Yea, from the cottage to the throne,
Hath magnified thy name!
From far Australia to Vancouver's pines,
From the High Alps to Russia's deepest mines,
From China, with her English lesson learnt,
To Chili, wailing for her daughters burnt;

There, everywhere, our Shakspeare breathes and moves
In the sweet ether of all human loves!—
Where rent America now writhes in woe,
Where Nile and Danube, Thames and Ganges flow,
Wherever England sails, and human kind
Anywhere feels in heart, and thinks in mind,
There, everywhere, our Shakspeare's voice is heard,
By him all souls are thrill'd, and cheer'd, and stirr'd;
Each passion flows or ebbs, as Shakspeare speaks,
Hate knits the brow, or terror pales the cheeks,
Love lights the eyes, or pity melts the heart,
And all men bow beneath our Poet's art!

VII.
What monument to rear,
What worthy offering?—
Nought lacks thy glory here
Of all thy sons can bring:
Long since, a twin-sphered brother spake,
How vain it were to raise
To such a Name, for Memory's sake,
Its pyramid of praise:
Our Shakspeare needs no sculptured stones,
No temple for his honoured bones!
But haply in his native street
Beside the rescued home
Hallowed by his infant feet
Whereto all pilgrims roam,
A College well might rear its head,
That Townsman's name to bear,
And brother-actors' sons he bred
To light and learning there!
And, for great London and its throngs,—
To Shakspeare of old right belongs
The Shakspeare Bridge, with Shakspeare scenes
Sculptured upon its pannell'd screens,
Colossus-like the Thames to span,
And telling every passing man
Where a poor player in his youth
Served Heaven and Earth by mimic truth,
And wrapped in Art's and Nature's robe,
Leased,— 'twas his Heritage, — the Globe!—

VIII.
Great Magician for all time,
Denizen of every clime,
Darling poet of mankind,
Master of the human mind,
Nature's very priest and king,—
Take the gifts thy children bring!
Let thy Spirit, hovering o'er

Thine earthly home and haunts of yore,
In its wisdom, wealth, and worth,
Shine upon us from above,
While thy kinsmen here on earth
Thus with pious care and love
Celebrate our Shakspeare's birth.

On The Site of A Mulberry-Tree; Planted By Wm. Shakspeare; Felled By The Rev. F. Gastrell by Dante Gabriel Rossetti

This tree, here fall'n, no common birth or death
Shared with its kind. The world's enfranchised son,
Who found the trees of Life and Knowledge one,
Here set it, frailer than his laurel-wreath.
Shall not the wretch whose hand it fell beneath
Rank also singly—the supreme unhung?
Lo! Sheppard, Turpin, pleading with black tongue
This viler thief's unsuffocated breath!
We'll search thy glossary, Shakspeare! whence almost,
And whence alone, some name shall be reveal'd
For this deaf drudge, to whom no length of ears
Sufficed to catch the music of the spheres;
Whose soul is carrion now,—too mean to yield
Some Starveling's ninth allotment of a ghost.

www.ingramcontent.com/pod-product-compliance
Lightning Source LLC
Chambersburg PA
CBHW071515040426
42444CB00008B/1657